This book will tool up the emerging usability professional, and will round out the experienced one. Karel, Scott, and Carol have done a great and thorough job of teaching the methods that define usability engineering, and of placing them in a meaningful context of organizational structures, finite development resources, political considerations, and communications challenges. This book demonstrates user-centered design to be a true and invaluable sub-discipline of software engineering, on par with programming, quality assurance, technical writing, marketing.

> Randolph G. Bias, Ph.D.
> Chief Usability Officer,
> Austin Usability

It has taken my company many years to develop a successful UCD/Usability program. Through years of trial and error, we developed, validated, and implemented many of the procedures and suggestions presented in this book. If this book were available at the start of our journey, we may have been able to develop a successful UCD/Usability program much more quickly and with much less pain. While most companies will need to modify the roadmap slightly to meet their own unique set of circumstances, it is, none-the-less an excellent foundation on which to build a solid UCD/Usability program.

> Jack Means
> Usability/Research Administrator
> Bloomington, Illinois.

If you are in the business of designing products or services that people use, and customer satisfaction is one of your critical objectives, then read this book. It provides a rich resource that will help both promote the UCD message, and implement sound "state of the art" practice.

> Ian McClelland
> Philips Consumer Electronics

For those who are committed to customer satisfaction, this book clearly spells out what to do, from the organization, to the project, to the individual level, to achieve products that work better for customers. It explains the realities of creating customer-centered products, under real business constraints. I'm sure that this book will not only be on our shelves, it will be recommended for all of our clients!

> Julie Nowicki
> President
> Optavia Corporation

OK, you've now proved there are usability problems with the products, and some of these usability problems stem from deeper problems with the business model and the way the organization is structured. This is the deeper challenge. Yes, you have the organization's interest for UCD, but it's a constant challenge to help the business units and the organization as a whole understand the unrealized value if it does not have UCD. I found this book very practical and helpful because it contains real-life business lessons learned that are useful to help you succeed in your organization.

Mary Lytwyn
Bank of Montreal

If usable products are your goal, then user-centered design is the only way to be sure to get there. This book will help you integrate and deploy user-centered design effectively in your organization.

Paul Eisen
Senior Consultant
Canadian Imperial Bank of Commerce

This is an immediately useful book that will help readers understand and introduce into their organizations a truly integrated UCD methodology. The book is filled with practical advice and tools based on the authors' real world experiences and insights. They so effectively emphasize the importance of a UCD approach that centers around user input and feedback and that employs a multidisciplinary team of diverse skills to design and develop the user's total experience—everything the user sees, hears, and touches.

Janice James
Founder and Past President
Usability Professionals' Association

UCD: An Integrated Approach is precisely the kind of accessible and pragmatic book about designing for usability that busy professionals need. Because it was written by people who have led the UCD charge from the trenches, this book offers the kinds of strategic insights and practical knowledge necessary for success in industry contexts. It's the kind of book that will sit comfortably next to *Cost-Justifying Usability* and *A Practical Guide to Usability* on my bookshelf. Because *UCD: An Integrated Approach* offers precisely the kind of practical, business-focused skill set I want graduate students in my usability testing seminar to develop, I certainly plan to use it in my courses.

Tharon Howard
UTEST Listowner
Clemson University Usability Testing Facility Director

A most welcome and timely addition to the field. Vredenburg, Isensee, and Righi combine to deliver over a quarter of a century of experience with User-Centered Design—and it shows. The book offers veteran insight to enable the professional to integrate UCD into the product development process while navigating the often-cloistered byways of corporate culture. The book's lessons learned and practical "how to" applications will certainly become a beneficial reference for students, practitioners, and managers alike.

Joseph E. Laviana, Ph.D.
Director, Worldwide Consumer Experience
Thomson Multimedia, Inc.

A broad and detailed examination of the essentials of User-Centered Design. This book covers the principles, the methods, and working examples you can use to build a successful UCD practice in your organization. It is a practical testimonial for following proven and well thought out practices for achieving strong alignment with user wants and needs in software development projects.

Edward Pierce
Director of Usability
Landmark Graphics, a Halliburton Company

Software Quality Institute Series

The Software Quality Institute Series is a partnership between the Software Quality Institute (SQI) at The University of Texas at Austin and Prentice Hall Professional Technical Reference (PHPTR). The books discuss real-life problems and offer strategies for improving software quality and software business practices.

Each publication is written by highly skilled, experienced practitioners who understand and can help solve the problems facing software professionals. SQI series topic areas include software development practices and technologies, management of software organizations, integration of high-quality software into other industries, business issues with reference to software quality, and related areas of interest.

TITLES IN THE SOFTWARE QUALITY INSTITUTE SERIES

USER-CENTERED DESIGN

An Integrated Approach

Karel Vredenburg, IBM
Scott Isensee, BMC Software
Carol Righi, Righi Interface Engineering

Software Quality Institute Series

PRENTICE HALL PTR
UPPER SADDLE RIVER, NJ 07458
WWW.PHPTR.COM

Library of Congress Cataloging-in-Publication Data

Vredenburg, Karel.
    User-centered design : an integrated approach / Karel Vredenburg, Scott Isensee, Carol Righi.
       p. cm. — (Software Quality Institute series)
    Includes bibliographical references and index.
    ISBN 0-13-091295-6 (pbk.)
    1. User interfaces (Computer systems) 2. Human engineering. 3. System design.
    I. Isensee, Scott. II. Righi, Carol. III. Title. IV. Series.
    QA76.9.U83 V74 2002
    004.2'1—dc21

                                   2001054871

Editorial/production supervision: *BooksCraft, Inc., Indianapolis, IN*
Acquisitions editor: *Paul Petralia*
Editorial assistant: *Richard Winkler*
Marketing manager: *Debby VanDijk*
Manufacturing manager: *Alexis R. Heydt-Long*
Cover design director: *Jerry Votta*
Cover designer: *Nina Scuderi*
Project coordinator: *Anne R. Garcia*
Technical reviewer: *Len Bullard*
Development editor:

**PH
PTR**

© 2002 by Prentice Hall PTR
Prentice-Hall, Inc.
Upper Saddle River, New Jersey 07458

ISBN 0-13-091295-6

Pearson Education Ltd.
Pearson Education Australia PTY. Ltd.
Pearson Education Singapore, Pte. Ltd.
Pearson Education North Asia Ltd.
Pearson Education Canada Ltd.
Pearson Educacion de Mexio, S.A. de C.V.
Pearson Education—Japan
Pearson Education Malaysia, Pte. Ltd.

Contents

Foreword

Picture the following scenario: A software development team is gathered around a table, in the early stages of planning for the design, development, and implementation of a software product. Let's say it is a piece of business software to run on a Windows platform. The discussion has been going on for a while, and there is much ambient excitement; it's a good idea and the team members know it.

> Marketing Director: "All of our market research says we're right on target with the functionality. Competitive intelligence tells us there's no competition on the immediate horizon. But the key to our success will be getting to the marketplace quickly."
>
> Product Director: "Great Bob. Mary, how long do you expect design and development will take?"
>
> Software Development Manager: "We've been talking about that, and we think we have a plan to hit the target window. By eliminating all software testing, we believe we can have this baby ready to launch in three months."

Now, what happens next? High-fives all around? Or does the director start going through her mental Rolodex for a replacement software development manager?

Likely it's the latter. For it would be folly to try to cut development corners by eliminating testing; way too many coding defects would probably cripple the effort and the product would be a disaster shortly after shipping.

For at least three decades now, User-Centered Design professionals have been admonishing product development teams to systematically gather and analyze user data as a routine part of development. "You budget time to debug the code and the hardware," goes the familiar plaint, "why not budget time to debug the design? Do you think designing is any easier, or less prone to error?" Sometimes the product development manager recognizes the importance of systematic, professional UCD, and sometimes it takes a disaster. It takes just one such disaster–a product that has wondrous functionality and is defect-free, but is a failure in the marketplace simply because people can't figure out how to carry out their tasks–to drive a product development manager to the joys of User-Centered Design.

Now that imaginary but, I hope, illustrative example may hold true for traditional computer products. But how about for the Web? Surely we don't need to worry about all this high-falutin' "User-Centered Design" approach if we're just building a Web site. Right?

Wrong. Indeed, four factors conspire to make a user-centered design approach even *more* important for Web sites and Web-based applications.

1. **Easy-to-use development tools open the field of "design" to more people.** The fact that I know how to use a hammer does not qualify me, let me assure you, to build a house. Just because someone has taken a short-course in HTML does not mean that that person can do a good job of designing Web pages. Now, I don't mean to imply that those who struggled to learn C++ are likely to be any better at design. It's just that now the population of "developers" is so much bigger, even more discernment is needed to identify those who are also good at design. And there are simply more "designs" out there (Web pages *ad infinitum*) that diverge from standards, to reflect a "designer's" joy of individuality, to frustrate the user who "just has a dang task to perform," and precious little time to perform it. I do *not* wish to imply that all software developers are bad designers. But when one looks, for example, at the software development curricula in colleges or at the wide array of Web sites that run from simple to use to "ohmigawd," one realizes that assuming all developers are good designers would be a bad bet—for the product development team and its investors.

2. **The time-to-market expectations for Web sites and Web apps are already anorexic, and on a diet.** Thanks to the aforementioned development tools, a person can get *some* web site up in, say, 20 minutes. Will it be useful? Will it be usable? Will any stray visitor likely return? These are all good questions. But there is a tendency for these questions to get buried in the noise, when the siren call of "how soon can you get the site up?" echoes through the development halls. When you are in a hurry, it is even *more* important to follow a (perhaps constrained, but intelligently selected) course of User-Centered Design, because, as I'll argue in the next paragraph, you may have only one chance.

3. **The expectations for Web sites are different than the expectations for traditional software applications.** Nobody but the serious propeller-

heads buys "Release 1" of any software product. Maybe, if you desperately needed the functionality, and were feeling a little saucy, you plunked down your money for Release 2. By the time Release 3 came out, you thought you'd give it a try, reasonably expecting the product not to crash your system or visit other unexpected events upon your computing life. For Web sites, you have one chance! When the buyer/information seeker can go next door with a single mouse click you had better make that first visit a positive experience. Web companies who expected to weed out the design bugs in the first release are, for the most part, ex-Web companies.

4. **Who the heck *are* our users out there?** When a company is selling system management software to big companies, it is a relatively easy matter (if it'll just take the time to do the research!) to find out who its users will be. They'll have a certain range of education, a certain range of experience at systems management tasks, perhaps a certain percentage will have had experience with a competitor's product or a predecessor product. When your Web site goes live, it can be accessed by, literally, *everyone*. (If, that is, you've made it accessible for folks with disabilities—see Chapter 2 for more.) Will your site be as usable by a 50-year-old female social worker in Austin as it will by a 14-year-old tennis player in Fiji? Should you care? For Web sites and Web-based applications it is imperative to understand who your target audience is and to test representative users to see if they find your site usable.

So far I have addressed two main themes:

- Designing is not easier than coding or building hardware, so you should budget time to debug your design, and
- This is even truer on the Web than it is with traditional hardware, software, and service products.

Let me add a third, before lauding Vredenburg, Isensee, and Righi for excellently addressing all three.

- **There is danger in "amateur User-Centered Design."**

If a person claims to be a programmer and is a poor one, this fact gets revealed fairly early in the engagement (certainly by the time of system test). If a person claims to be a UCD engineer and is a poor one, this fact may not be revealed until the customer support team is inundated with calls, or the Web site has had hundreds of thousands of visitors ("thanks to that excellent marketing campaign we spent so much on") only to have 95% of them leave before making their intended purchase because they couldn't figure out how to navigate the site.

UCD is not rocket science, but it's not common sense, either. There are universities that offer Master's and Ph.D. programs in human-computer interaction, usability engineering, and related fields, but because of the rapid evolution of these fields, there's no universally accepted curriculum. And while there is a Board that certifies Human Factors Professionals and Professional Ergonomists, an important goal for such a certifying body is still to get businesses to understand the importance and value of a solid base of professional expertise and to hire and assign based on that understanding. And so the development manager who is interested in hiring a User-Centered Design expert, or the technical writer who wishes to become a UCD practitioner, or the product development team that wishes to implement a full course of User-Centered Design, all have uncertain paths before them.

They all will gain clarity about their path if they read this book. Vredenburg, Isensee, and Righi are, individually and as a team, a rare mix. They have all spent years in the usability and UCD trenches, being absolute models of how to support software products empirically, creatively, and cost effectively. (I have had the pleasure of working directly with each of them and so have firsthand data on this matter.) Also, they have all trained others, in formal classes, in conference tutorials, and as informal mentors. And they have shared their wisdom with the field via conference presentations, books, and technical articles. Among them, they have a combined 50+ years carrying out, inventing, managing, proselytizing, training, and documenting UCD methods. This book represents a crisp, readable, actionable distillation of all their accumulated knowledge about the invaluable design approach that is User-Centered Design.

I've said that the authors are expert at conducting and teaching UCD methods, and that's true. But this book—as suggested by its subtitle, "An Integrated Approach"—is more than a series of how-to chapters. Their presentation of an "integrated approach" includes some historical perspective (as they help you anticipate the "Yeah, buts" you're likely to hear). It offers time-tested advice on driving user-centered design into your organization, on cost-justifying (quantifiably) your usability expenditures, on good communication in order to drive awareness throughout your organization. With pedagogic tools like case studies (many illustrative case studies!), FAQs, and an included CD with tools for the practitioner, they not only present the content, but demonstrate their sincerity about "tooling up" the emerging UCD practitioner or software development team.

I believe the key to successfully kicking off a User-Centered Design approach, or to becoming a successful UCD practitioner, is discernment. It is important to discern *what* sorts of user data are needed *when* in the development cycle. It is important to discern *which* methods to employ to gather those data. It is important to discern *who* to pursue as test participants, *how* to carry out the evaluations, and *how* to apply these data to design. And it is important to discern which methods the emerging usability engineer, or the team just now pursuing a User-Centered Design approach, might likely carry out successfully, and which to save for the experienced professional. This book will clearly communicate to both the emerging and experienced UCD practitioner, manager, or other IT professional what he or she doesn't know, and what he or she needs to know, and will go a long way towards bridging that gap.

A few months ago I attended an open house for a software development company that makes and sells wireless computing applications. I sought out the director of user interface design, with the intent of selling her some systematic usability engineering services. She was a pleasant person and welcomed my informal sales pitch. However, she said they already "did" UCD. "Oh, yes. I show the interface around to everyone in the office before we ship." I tried a little harder to convince her of the importance of a systematic, professional UCD approach, and she listened politely. By this point in the evening we were both out of business cards. "Here," she said brightly, "I'll just email you on my phone, using our new product, and then we'll both have each other's contact information." I said that would be great, and spoke aloud my email address. Ten minutes and many grimaces later she *thought* she had successfully sent one email. If they're still in business, I will send her a copy of *User-Centered Design: An Integrated Approach*.

Randolph G. Bias, Ph.D.
Austin Usability
Austin, TX
August, 2001

Preface

Do you want to change what people say about your product or system, referring to it as "elegant, simple, and powerful" rather than "ham-fisted, ugly, and unusable"? Or perhaps they're not saying anything at all. Then this book is for you. It provides an integrated approach to User-Centered Design (UCD) with an emphasis on using UCD to make products easy to buy, learn, and use. It focuses on designing a compelling "total customer experience" — everything a customer sees, hears, and touches about a product or system.

The integrated version of User-Centered Design, described in this book, was initially developed at IBM in the early 1990s by Karel Vredenburg. A team of experts at IBM continuously worked with the first author to improve this version of UCD. It is currently in its third major version. Scott Isensee and Carol Righi were instrumental in the evolution of the approach not only while they were at IBM but also after they left the company. Since leaving IBM, Scott has applied UCD effectively to the design of the i-opener information appliance at NetPliance and currently implements UCD at BMC Software. Carol formed her own company, Righi Interface Engineering, Inc. She has led UCD projects both while at IBM and now as a consultant for clients such as Chrysler, MetLife, and the Usability Professionals' Association and has taught User-Centered Design classes to major corporations. We continue to run a highly popular workshop entitled, "How to Introduce, Deploy, and Optimize User-Centered Design in Your Organization."

This book is a distillation of our collective experience and that of our colleagues in introducing UCD to many hundreds of companies and deploying it on a few thousand projects over the past 10 years. We have used the approach to design products ranging from mainframe computers to integrated circuits, notebook computers to Web appliances, database software to speech recognition software, Web site portals to the Web site for the Olympics, and we have used it on consulting projects worldwide for many industries, including healthcare, finance and banking, aerospace, insurance, automotive, and retail.

We sincerely hope that you enjoy reading the book and applying the information contained within it.

Acknowledgments

The process of defining and implementing integrated UCD has involved many people. As the process continues to become an ever more important part of the way products are developed, more people are becoming involved. The people who practice UCD every day are making it a success. Special thanks goes to John Schwarz for providing Karel Vredenburg 6 months and a team with whom to develop UCD at IBM, Hershel Harris for leading the first successful UCD project, Al Zollar for helping to drive the first companywide UCD communications campaign, Steve Mills for recognizing the importance of UCD to the IBM software development and his support ever since, Lou Gerstner for the insight to drive UCD across all of IBM, and Tony Temple and Susan Mills for their continued leadership and support of the Ease of Use program at IBM. The IBM UCD Advisory Council, a group of approximately 30 discipline leaders and divisional UCD leaders from across the company, has made significant technical contributions to UCD. We can't mention everyone, but we would like to acknowledge a few people who have had the most substantial technical influence: Paul W. Smith, Mike Fischer, Julian Jones, Bob Jones, Frank Eldredge, Carolyn Bjerke, Rick Herder, John Boscarino, Simon Hakiel, Ken Stern, John Karat, Jim Lewis, Mike Stokes, Linda Liebelt, Dirk Willuhn, Mike DiAngelo, Charlotte Schwendeman, Paul McInerney, Dick Berry, Alan Tannenbaum, and Colin Powell. Case study information was contributed by Michael Boshes, Robert Atlas, Tony Haverda, Karen Lefave, Lynn VanDyke, Marion Radin, and Diane Wilson.

In addition to our coworkers, our peers at other companies have generously contributed tips from their experience and reviewed this manuscript to assure us that the advice we give is broadly applicable and accurate.

We are grateful to our students and development team members who have challenged our assumptions, prompted us to explain more clearly, and helped us to practice UCD on the UCD process itself. UCD is more efficient and practical because of it.

Thanks to the reviewers who provided many helpful comments and suggestions on this book.

Thanks most of all to our families, Erin O'Brien; Elliot, Emma, Rowan, and Noah Vredenburg; Dawn Isensee; and Rob and Sarah Ripperdan for their love and support during the writing of this book.

Introduction

User-Centered Design (UCD) makes products easy to use. Unfortunately, making products easy can be hard work. The goal of this book is to reveal the techniques we have found to be successful in developing and implementing a UCD program.

Markets for most products are becoming more competitive. Products that have unacceptable usability typically do not survive. Customers are demanding usable products. At the same time that customer expectations are rising, developers are being challenged to produce products on shorter schedules at lower cost. In this environment, techniques that are very efficient and effective are needed. The techniques discussed in this book are meeting that challenge at IBM and many other companies.

This book is written for the broad range of UCD professionals. For those who are new to the field or are starting a UCD program in an organization, it outlines the best approaches for introducing UCD. For those who are experts in the field or for organizations with mature UCD programs, it provides ways to optimize your implementation of UCD.

The purpose of this book is not to provide a comprehensive usability engineering handbook; nor is it intended to teach you how to "do design." Rather, this book is intended to complement those skill-oriented volumes that offer those approaches by providing practical advice on how to prepare for, deploy, and optimize an overall UCD approach into an organization.

Chapter 1 provides information that you can use to take stock of your current organization's position regarding the core elements of UCD. Chapter 2 summarizes the various aspects of our integrated approach. The critically important step of introducing UCD to your organization is the focus of Chapter 3, and Chapter 4 provides a detailed account of how to deploy and carry out UCD. Chapter 5 examines various ways to optimize your deployment of UCD with a variety of tools and technologies and discusses future trends in methodology and technology integration. The book contains numerous case studies that describe how UCD was used in real-life projects, from small applications intended for in-house use to large-scale consumer products intended for a worldwide market. The bibliography provides additional resources beyond the material in the chapters. In addition, a CD with useful information, Web site links, and tools is included at the back of the book.

We recommend that you read the book from Chapter 1 through to Chapter 5. However, to facilitate the use of the book as a reference, we designed each chapter to stand alone to a certain degree. If you have read the entire book and now want to start to introduce your organization to UCD, you should proceed to Chapter 2 directly. Also, if you are an experienced UCD practitioner and are interested in optimizing your deployment of UCD, you may want to proceed directly to Chapter 5, skimming the preceding chapters as necessary.

Given that we practice User-Centered Design in everything we do, we are very interested in getting feedback from you, the book's users. When you are finished with the book, we would appreciate it if you would visit the Web site address *www.righiinterface.com/ucd/survey* to complete a brief survey about your experience with the book.

This book provides best practice based on our experience developing and implementing a UCD program at IBM and numerous other companies at which we have worked and for whom we have consulted. We hope that you will find the information in this book to be useful in helping to transform and/or optimize your own organization.

Taking Stock

Most organizations today understand, or at least give lip service to, the need to design products and systems that are easy to use and meet the requirements of their intended audience. Few companies, however, understand how to go about designing usable products and systems. The approach for doing this is User-Centered Design (UCD).

This chapter will help you take stock of key elements of your company's current opportunities to incorporate UCD. The following chapters will then provide an overview of our integrated UCD approach, offer guidance with the introduction and deployment of it, and summarize ways to optimize it with advanced technologies and methods.

To move to a UCD approach, you must understand your company's current design approach and the changes needed to move to UCD. The current design approach will vary from one company to another, but a number of elements are common to many companies. In these instances, companies are using the traditional approach (see Figure 1.1).

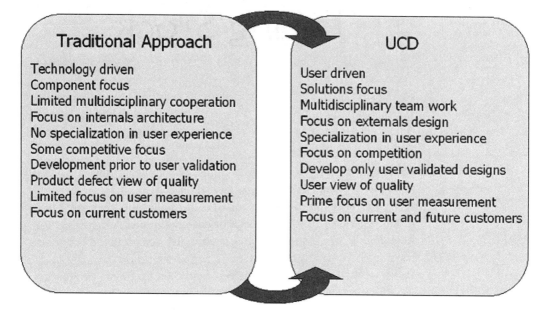

FIGURE 1.1
Contrasting the traditional approach to design with UCD.

The UCD approach differs from the traditional approach in the following ways:

- **Technology/user driven.** The most obvious difference between the traditional approach and the UCD approach concerns the involvement of customers. Traditional approaches are fundamentally technology driven. Although they may collect customer requirements at the start of a project, they gather little or no input from users during the design and development process itself. Design is typically *inside-out;* that is, the internal architecture is defined first and then a user interface is created for users to get access to the system functions. In contrast, UCD is fundamentally user driven. Customers are involved in all stages of design and development. The customer experience is designed first, and then product or system architecture is created to support this design. In other words, UCD is design that is *outside-in.* Note that this focus does not occur just during design and development. Rather, all aspects of the product are customer driven: features, packaging, advertising, appearance, user interface, ordering process, user assistance, and support. Customer input guides the design of the total customer experience.

- **Component/Solutions focus.** Traditionally, products such as software applications have been viewed as a collection of components—bits of code that execute certain functions. This view places the user in a role secondary to that of the technology. A solutions focus, on the other hand, views an application as a tool, perhaps one of several, that helps a user accomplish a set of tasks. The emphasis is not on the technology per se, but on the user and his or her tasks.

- **Multidisciplinary work.** Traditional product development usually involves "specialists" who work on their own. Late in the design process, the pieces are brought together into a single package. Unfortunately, because these specialists often have limited interaction during design and development, they frequently encounter disconnects in their visions for the product, their implementation, and the like. The result of such an approach is often a product that looks as though different factions created its different pieces. UCD, on the other hand, is defined by a strong multidisciplinary emphasis. A team of specialists (see Figure 1.2) works closely together throughout the process so that everyone is working toward the same goal. Consequently, the resulting product appears to the customer as if a single team, all thinking alike, designed and developed the solution.

- **Internal/external design.** Most development organizations that use the traditional approach focus primarily on internals architecture and code development. Project design and status meetings focus on code implementation. On the other hand, UCD focuses first and foremost on the product from the user's perspective. Design meetings are characterized by the desire to create a positive customer experience and to find ways to use technology to achieve this end. Status meetings examine key UCD metrics, together with code-related ones, to get a complete picture of the project.

- **Specialization.** Key specialists in traditional organizations including software architecture and software engineering personnel; they are typically the most influential and powerful individuals in the organization. However, in an organization practicing UCD, the software architecture and engineering disciplines are equivalent to other key disciplines such as visual design, human-computer interaction design, and user assistance architecture. In fact, IBM (Vredenburg, 2001) created a new role that is responsibile for the total customer experience design and leads the various disciplines in achieving it.

- **Competitive focus.** Most traditional approaches involve collecting requirements and translating them into product design. Targets for such things as time to install are often determined by estimating or guessing. UCD, in contrast, focuses on using the competition as the target. Competition in this context refers to the ways in which the majority of customers currently accomplish the specified tasks. If a competitor's product has the majority market share, that is the competition. If, on the other hand, there is no current competitor and no computer-based solution exists, then the analogue method is the competition. For example, Visicalc, the first spreadsheet program, had to beat the paper-and-pencil spreadsheet techniques that were used before it. The primary way of doing a task today should form the comparison and benchmark for the design and development effort. Specifying a target for time to install using UCD involves examining the primary competitive solution to determine its installation time, determining customer satisfaction with this information, and then specifying a target based on this information, together with the overall objective regarding how much better the product is attempting to be than current competitive solution.

- **Validation.** Traditional approaches to design and development often do not include any user validation. In fact, first customer ship is often the *only* user validation. With this approach, one version of the product is the prototype for the next version. Of course, if it takes 10 iterations or prototypes to get the design right, that means 10 versions of the product, which may mean 5 to 10 years of development effort, assuming that customers will wait that long for a product to finally meet their needs. In traditional approaches, if user validation of designs is done, it is carried out after code has been written and often when the product design and implementation is virtually complete. Of course, little or no change to the product can be made at this point in the development cycle without significant expense and time. By contrast, user input is central to UCD, and user validation of design occurs iteratively throughout the design and development cycle. The first versions of the design shown to customers are created with pencil and paper and, therefore, are extremely inexpensive and quick to change. Subsequent higher fidelity prototypes that customers evaluate are also comparatively inexpensive and quick to change. Final versions of the design are implemented in code and in other aspects of the product and are as expensive and difficult to change as those developed using traditional methods; however, very few changes are typically required given all the user input gathered up to that point.

- **View of Quality.** Quality in most traditional approaches to design and development is understood to mean the lack of technical defects, such as code defects, that have an impact on the reliability of the product. Some companies go to great lengths to drive these types of defects down to zero, often at the expense of other aspects of quality. In addition, organizations that follow traditional approaches often discount problems encountered by customers. If the product works as designed, the problem is not logged as a defect and instead is recorded as "user error" or "working as designed." Little or nothing is ever done about problems in the latter category. Instead, UCD focuses on quality as specified by the customer. In fact, if users cannot proceed to complete a critical task using the product even though the product is working perfectly with regard to reliability, it must be fixed before the product is shipped. The focus on the customer view of quality ensures that products and systems not only work the way customers expect them to but also work at the level of reliability that is desired.

- **User measurements.** In traditional approaches, benchmarks, throughput, and the like are the most important measurements. Customer measurements are seen as subjective, and not as useful. In UCD, customer measurements are primary because the customers define whether a product is successful. Core UCD measurements can be taken at various points throughout a design and development cycle as input to design and as in-process indicators for project management.

- **Customers.** The "voice of the customer" approaches championed by some traditional approaches focus on gathering input from existing customers, even when the product concerned may have garnered only 5% market share. Although satisfying current customers is fine, in this example, 95% of the market was voting with its pocketbook against the current product and in favor of one or more competitors. UCD focuses, instead, on customers in the entire market segment, including those currently using a competitor's product, those making the purchase decision, and the eventual end user. In this way, the product is designed for the entire market. Key design characteristics that customers of competitive products would like to see are included as well.

| Total user experience leader | Marketing specialist | Visual/Industrial designer | Human-computer interaction designer | User assistance architect |

| Technology architect | Service and support specialist | User research specialist | Internationalization/ Terminology specialist | UCD Project leader |

FIGURE 1.2
Multidisciplinary design team. (Photographs courtesy of PhotoDisc.)

Your Current Organization and Products

Assessing your current organization and products will help you determine where to start your UCD efforts.

You need to determine the degree of support available in your organization for adopting UCD. Although it is possible to start UCD as a grassroots effort, you are much more likely to be successful if you have sponsorship and support from senior management. They control funding and have the ability to influence others throughout the company. If you don't have this support initially, you may be able to foster it through informing the "movers and shakers" in your company about the benefits of UCD.

You also need to assess the support and knowledge of your coworkers, especially those from the various disciplines represented in the UCD approach (e.g., developers, marketing specialists, writers). If they support UCD, it will be much easier to adopt UCD. If they are initially unknowledgable about or even hostile to UCD, your job will be much more difficult. You may be able to win them over by educating them about UCD and demonstrating its value, but this is usually a gradual process. A better approach is to have their support up front.

In addition to being open to UCD, the development teams must also be knowledgable about it. Everyone practices UCD, not just usability specialists. Everyone involved in the design and development of products needs to know about UCD and have the skills required to practice it at the appropriate level.

The current level of usability of your products also affects the degree of impact UCD will have. The more usability problems there are, the more opportunity for improvement. There may be "low hanging fruit" or problems which can be fixed easily and show obvious progress. The degree to which usability is demanded by your customers also affects your opportunity for success with UCD. There is often strong demand for usability in consumer products, for example, because the customer will choose a competing product if it is easier to use. There may be less demand for usability in internally developed applications because there is no competition and users may have become resigned to accepting whatever they are told to use.

You also must determine the degree of support for institutionalizing UCD in your organization. A few enthusiasts practicing UCD on their coffee breaks won't get you very far. You need the right people with the right skills and they need to be given the time and resources necessary to do a good job. The company also needs to commit to formally integrating UCD activities within the development process. UCD activities need to be included in project plans. If UCD activities are not an official part of a project, they are usually reduced to "too little too late."

Finally, you must determine what each part of your organization wants. People and projects differ, so it is difficult to implement a one-size-fits-all UCD program. UCD can be modular and flexible; consequently, it can be tailored to the needs and realities of a particular project.

CASE STUDY: CLARIFYING PROJECT OBJECTIVES FROM THE START

- Assess consensus on project objectives.
- Make your data usable.
- Communicate results upward.

We consulted on a project for a developer of insurance policy tracking software. The company wanted to convert their text-based application interface to a graphical user interface (GUI). After we arrived on site, we quickly observed that the product objectives seemed to change almost daily and to differ as a function of who related them. The president of the company, however, was not aware that such a situation existed. Rather than simply meet with him and offer what could have been perceived as our opinion, we conducted a brief survey to assess the staff's perceptions and understanding of the objectives for the new product. Most of the survey questions asked for a rating of agreement with a stated product objective (e.g., "Move into the medium- and large-company market" and "Add more function to compete with other systems in the market"). Agreement was measured on a five-point scale, with a one being "Strongly Disagree" and a five being "Strongly Agree." Respondents were asked to comment on each rating. Other questions asked for such information as, "Who will be your prime competitor over the next 12 months?" The survey was distributed to all key staff (about 10 people). (Because the survey was of a population, and not a sample, results were valid even though only 10 people were surveyed.)

The survey results confirmed our observations. We compiled the results and wrote a brief summary in text rather than numerical form, so that management would view these results as tangible, usable information, not as an academic exercise. For example, we wrote,

> There was general agreement that the following objectives are fairly important: Moving into the medium- and large-company market, and retaining the business of small companies by allowing an adaptable GUI. There was very little agreement regarding whether adding new function is important and in identifying the prime competitor.

As a consequence of this survey and other evidence of the lack of a clear, shared direction, the company postponed the project until it could set forth objectives and agree upon the key issues.

Although this particular type of survey will likely not be found in a typical collection of UCD methods, it was clearly in the interest of the project to gather objective data regarding the staff's lack of agreement regarding product objectives and to bring these data to the attention of upper management. It is critical that the management team and design team be in synch with regard to objectives before design begins. Rather than sweep differences under the rug in the hopes they would be resolved without intervention, it is important to instead bring them to light, and allow discussion and resolution to occur prior to starting to design.

> Most companies have insufficient skills available to practice UCD in the design of all of their products. This is particularly true when UCD is first being introduced into a company. You must access your opportunities and pick the ones which have the greatest chance of success and provide the biggest bang for the buck.

We have had the best effect by first practicing UCD on products which:

- Are recognized as having poor total customer experiences
- Can be improved with a reasonable amount of time and effort
- Are important products to the company so that improvements will have substantial effect and be noticed
- Are early in the design or re-design phase
- Have a team willing or even eager to try UCD

Your Preliminary Road Map

Nielsen (1993) recommended the following five-point plan to increase usability in an organization:

1. Recognize the need for usability in the organization.
2. Make it clear that usability has management support.
3. Devote specific resources to usability engineering.
4. Integrate systematic usability engineering activities into various stages of the development life cycle.
5. Make sure that all user interfaces are subjected to user testing.

These same points can be applied to increasing an organization's focus on the total customer experience (Vredenburg, 1999). Specifically, we have found the following to be key success factors in the UCD roadmap.

- **Prepare organization.** The organization must be ready to accept and embrace UCD. Like people, organizations must admit that they have a problem before they can work toward a solution.

- **Ensure alignment from practitioner to executive.** Hiring a usability specialist is not sufficient to create a compelling total customer experience. All members of a multidisciplinary development team should practice UCD. It requires knowledge and support by the entire management chain, from the practitioners up through the executives. The practitioners can come up with the ideas, but the executives are often needed to make sure that those ideas are implemented.

- **Develop new roles.** To facilitate effective implementation and practice of UCD, special roles need to be defined. These new roles include an executive with companywide responsibility for UCD such as the Ease of Use Vice President at IBM, Ease of Use Champions who serve as advocates of usability in each business unit, and Ease of Use Architects who provide high-level direction. These roles will be described in more detail in later chapters.

- **Educate executives, managers, practitioners.** Knowledge of UCD needs to be widely disseminated throughout the organization. Management needs UCD education as much as the practitioners.

- **Establish corporate targets.** Targets or goals to motivate people to improve and to measure progress against are essential.

- **Review progress and provide consultancy help.** Simply teaching a development team about UCD usually isn't sufficient. Ideally, a knowledgable, experienced UCD practitioner should be assigned to the team. If that is not feasible, then a UCD professional should periodically review the progress of the team and provide assistance on a consulting basis.

- **Start at grassroots — lab to corporate.** Most successful UCD programs have started as a grassroots effort. UCD is practiced on some small projects, and, when success has been demonstrated, management can be convinced to support applying UCD more pervasively throughout the organization. At IBM, the UCD program started at a single development lab, spread to other labs, and was eventually implemented companywide, coordinated by an organization at the corporate level.

- **Define UCD broadly — total customer experience.** UCD is most successful if it is defined broadly. Rather than designing just the user interface for the product, UCD should be practiced to optimize the total customer experience for the product. (See Figure 1.3.)

- **Establish multilevel views — principles, process, tools.** If UCD is to be practiced effectively and efficiently, a support structure needs to be in place. Materials that can support a successful UCD program include guiding principles, a UCD process integrated with the company's development process, and tools that help practitioners perform UCD activities.

- **Reduce cycle time/resource.** Most companies are under great pressure to do more with less. UCD, likewise, must become more efficient. Even though the perception that UCD activities add time and expense to product development exists, the opposite is true. UCD facilitates developing products with an understanding of customer needs early on, which saves rework later in the development process.

Everything the customer sees, hears, and touches

Order   Get   Unpack
Find   Install
Upgrade   Use
Support   Help

FIGURE 1.3
The total customer experience. (Courtesy of IBM.)

- **Start with a pilot project.** It is wise to deploy UCD in a pilot project before rolling it out across the board. A pilot project will give you a chance to work out any initial problems with your implementation of UCD and demonstrate the value of UCD.

- **Establish UCD as an internal brand and advertise it.** Companies should treat UCD as they would any other marketing campaign. They should seek to raise awareness of what UCD is, in part, through advertising. (See Figures 1.4 and 1.5.) There should be incentives to development teams to practice UCD. One technique is to provide a process by which products can become UCD certified to demonstrate that they are usable.

- **Communicate successes companywide.** Let the company know about UCD successes. UCD teams can't implement something they haven't heard about. Make sure that the whole company is aware of UCD and hears about successes.

- **Review feedback on approach.** Practice UCD on UCD. The process should continuously evolve and improve.

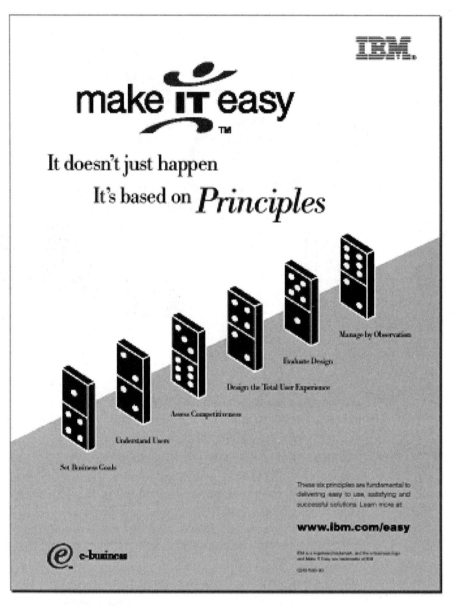

FIGURE 1.4
IBM advertises UCD through a series of promotional materials. (Courtesy of IBM.)

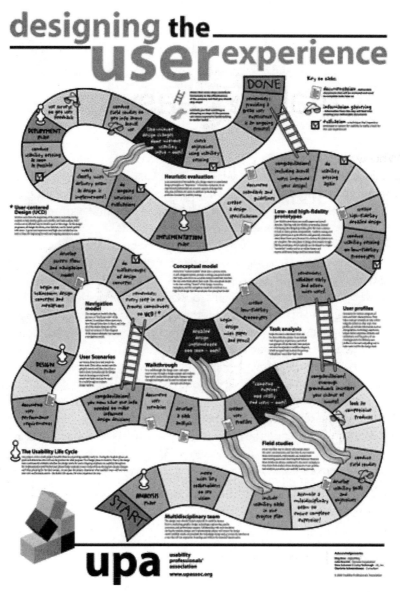

FIGURE 1.5

Poster of the UCD process designed and distributed by the Usability Professionals'
Association. (Courtesy of the Usability Professionals' Association [Copyright UPA 2000].)

CASE STUDY: SPREADING THE WORD ABOUT UCD

- Many long-time employees of large companies may need to be convinced that UCD is "not just another process."
- Both organizational leaders and staff must be enlisted in the effort to integrate UCD into an organization.
- To be recognized as a formal organizational process, UCD should be documented as such.

When we introduced the UCD process at the development site of a large multinational company a few years ago, the usability department made every attempt to integrate UCD into existing lab software development practices. The manager of the department developed and implemented a strategy. First, she educated other development managers about UCD. This task posed quite a challenge. Over the years, many large organizations that have been around for a long time had introduced and implemented many development processes. Many of these had their day in the sun but soon fell out of practice. Because of this precedent, the usability manager's most important job was to convince those who had been through many reengineering efforts that UCD was not just another process. Her efforts along these lines were pervasive and tenacious. She presented UCD at numerous area and division meetings. She simultaneously practiced a grassroots approach and a trickle-down approach to spreading the word so that virtually everyone at the lab at least heard about UCD. She held regular UCD status meetings with the leaders of the various product development disciplines, including the lead software architect, the marketing brand manager, and the head of service and support. She helped the respective departments integrate UCD into the various ongoing software projects and became involved in documenting the UCD process for the organization's efforts at preparing for certification by the International Standards Organization (ISO).

Dealing with the "Yeah, Buts..." _____

Many people like to maintain the status quo. They will resist moving from the traditional approach they are comfortable with to a new, UCD approach. The benefits of UCD are hard to deny, but they may try to find reasons why it won't work in their particular organization. They will try to find excuses not to change. We call these excuses the *yeah, buts*. Here are some of the common excuses we have encountered and our responses to them.

But Making Usable Products Is Expensive

Making products and interactive systems more user-centered saves money. It has substantial business and personal benefits. Products and systems that are more usable

- Are easier to understand and use, thus reducing training and support costs;
- Reduce discomfort and stress and improve customer satisfaction;
- Improve the productivity of users and the operational efficiency of organizations;
- Improve product quality, aesthetics, and impact;
- Can provide a competitive advantage.

The complete benefits of user-centered design come from calculating the total life-cycle costs of the product including conception, design, implementation, support, use, and maintenance. Bias and Mayhew (1994) provided methods for calculating these benefits and case studies from development projects at several companies. Typically UCD techniques not only return several times their cost in savings to the company developing the software but also provide benefits to companies or users purchasing the software.

Recently, we conducted a survey that showed usability as one of the top three most critical characteristics that customers expect of modern products. Even though it is related to other aspects of product quality, usability is most strongly related to overall product customer satisfaction.

But We Have a Schedule to Meet

The UCD approach often saves time on a project. Time is, of course, spent finding and fixing customer-perceived problems, but UCD emphasizes early identification of problems, which allows the problems to be fixed while changes are still relatively easy. Changes late in development are typically several times more expensive than the same changes made earlier. Changes that must be made after the product is already in the hands of the customers are particularly expensive both in terms of dollar cost and impact on sales.

But Our Users Care More About ...

This sentence can be completed with "price," "performance," "features," or any of a number of other attributes. Sometimes it is true, but most often it is not. The truth is that few development teams really know what their customers want most. It is important to gather this information and make informed trade-off decisions.

But We Only Have a Small Team

UCD is a scalable process. We recognize that the activities performed when the team or project size is small cannot and should not be the same as when it is large. UCD is like exercise: You may never do as much as you should, but every little bit helps. Many companies start with the low-hanging fruit. They implement the UCD activities that have the biggest payback first and then add more as they are able.

CASE STUDY: PROVING THAT UCD WORKS

- Asking product managers to trust that UCD will work is not enough.

- Real-world examples of product success and failure with UCD can help win some support.

- Examples that are close to home help the most.

Most interface designers and usability engineers have encountered the skepticism of product managers, developers, and others when attempting to implement UCD. Asking these individuals to "just trust me" doesn't gain their support. Instead, they say, "Show me." Unfortunately, most of us do not have the luxury of running controlled experiments on the products we're developing. How can you prove that UCD works? We have used many different examples to convince others of the efficacy of UCD. Among these examples are the following.

- **"Flops" stories.** Relate stories of real products that have failed in the marketplace because they did not meet the needs of their intended users — in short, failure due to lack of UCD. Examples include the New Coke, Reynolds's smokeless cigarette, and dry beer. (See Figure 1.6.)

- **Success stories.** Conversely, relate real-world examples of successful UCD efforts. If possible, use examples of products developed within the company or by a direct competitor that have succeeded because they employed a UCD approach to create an engaging total customer experience. For example, the Miata's engine was supposedly made louder after early tests revealed that customers thought it was too quiet for a sports car. Examples of successful information technology (IT) UCD stories include the IBM DB2 Universal Database, and the PalmPilot. Non-IT examples include the Miata, Volkswagen, and Disney experience.

- **The product itself.** Although it's usually not possible to run full-scale experiments in a product development environment, small pieces of the product (e.g., a particular feature) can be demonstrated before and after user involvement and multidisciplinary attention are applied. Objective measurements can give the example further legitimacy.

Flops!

I Many product have failed due to poor user experiences

   I Women's perfume marketed as a cigarette lighter: Not very appealing to consumers

   I Dry beer: Confused consumers did not know what it was

   I Smokeless cigarettes: Smokers **like** smoke!

   I "Virucidal tissues" scared consumers!

FIGURE 1.6
Know Thy User!

The Integrated Approach 2

Integrated UCD designs ease of use into the total customer experience with products and systems. It involves two fundamental elements: multidisciplinary teamwork and a set of specialized methods of acquiring user input and converting it into design.

UCD involves design specialists from several disciplines, such as marketing, human-computer interaction, visual/industrial design, user assistance design, technology architecture engineering, service/support, and user research (often called human factors engineering). It ensures that a disciplined, integrated, customer-based process is used throughout the design and development of offerings and solutions. This process includes the following types of activities:

- Understanding users' activities, which provide an understanding of the customers, their environment, the tasks they currently perform, and the tasks they anticipate performing in the future;

- Designing and evaluating design activities, which facilitate the conceptual and detailed design of the offering and evaluate the design iteratively with users;

- Assessing competitiveness activities, which assess the offering design relative to the prime competitor's offering design.

This chapter introduces the central concepts of UCD, describes the central principles of UCD, and provides an overview of UCD methods and techniques.

What's in a Name?

The *user* in UCD refers to the person who will be using the product or system being built. Some people argue for alternatives to this designation, including *customer, learner,* or just *human.* In fact, a particular term appears to be in "style" for a year or two until a new one comes into vogue among practitioners. Although these changes in vocabulary may suit the needs of practitioners or others for whom these nuances are important, it is often confusing to nonpractitioners who consequently no longer recognize the approach. We tend to use the terms *user* and *customer* interchangeably. The *centered* part of UCD refers to the fact that aspects of UCD revolve around one center, the user. The *design* in UCD refers to the creation of the total customer experience. The *D* part of UCD can also stand for discovery, definition, development, and delivery.

How Is Our Integrated Approach to UCD Unique?

Because the term *UCD* has been used to describe a generic approach to product development, many flavors of UCD exist in the industry. Most current versions of UCD, including the one described in this book, have their origins in the seminal work of Norman and Draper (1986). This book introduced the basic terminology and some of the central ideas of this approach to product development. Building on this foundation, a number of unique enhancements were built into our version of UCD to make it integrated, scalable, and fast. Integrated UCD is unique among design approaches in several important ways:

- Integrated UCD deals with the design of the total customer experience from the first time a potential customer sees an ad about a product or service through the time he or she would like to upgrade to a new version. The focus of other versions of UCD is typically much more limited. They only focus on the graphical user interface itself, in the case of software, or such things as the computer keyboard, in the case of hardware. To achieve the focus on the total customer experience, inte-

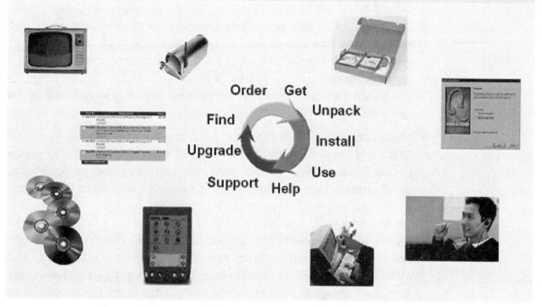

Everything the customer sees, hears, and touches

Order　Get

Find　Unpack

Upgrade　Install

Support　Use

Help

FIGURE 2.1
The total customer experience. (Courtesy of IBM.)

grated UCD uses a multidisciplinary team of diverse skills to design everything the customer sees, hears, and touches (see Figure 2.1).

- Integrated UCD uses a variety of techniques from heavy-duty to lightweight and specifies when each is required. Not all projects are the same; therefore, UCD doesn't have a one-size-fits-all solution. A careful study of the variation in projects has yielded a set of project profiles and the methods and techniques appropriate to each. In this book, we incorporated both industry-standard techniques and new techniques that we developed ourselves, specifying where each is appropriate.

- The process focuses on affective as well as cognitive and behavioral aspects of a customer's interaction with an offering. In other words, it ensures that customers are delighted with an offering, beyond not experiencing major problems using it.

- Measurements taken throughout the project are a key element of integrated UCD. Many industry practitioners believe that ease of use and related attributes cannot be measured or managed. We disagree. We have developed an extensive set of measurements that are taken throughout a project to help identify problems and make midcourse corrections. These provide a powerful means for managing projects so that they will satisfy customers.

- Integrated UCD has been optimized with state-of-the-art tools and technologies. In many cases, UCD activities as practiced elsewhere in the industry are time consuming and labor intensive. Integrated UCD, on the other hand, includes a set of tools that turbocharge our methods and techniques. Activities that used to take days and weeks now take a few minutes.

- Many companies know that they need to use a process like integrated UCD, but they don't know how to get started. We've developed a package for getting started including introductory presentations, development team education classes, executive education workshops, and consulting services to get a project started quickly.

  Integrated UCD has benefited greatly from other published works (Hamel and Prahalad, 1989; Norman and Draper, 1986; Wiklund, 1994) and from our collective experience carrying out integrated UCD and other versions of UCD (Vredenburg, 2001). Integrated UCD also was improved drawing from the work of industry peers in the American Computer Machinery Special Interest Group for Computer Human Interaction (SIGCHI), the Usability Professionals' Association (UPA), and the Human Factors and Ergonomics Society (HFES) conferences, as well as standards organizations such as the International Standards Organization (ISO) and the U.S. National Institute for Standards and Technology (NIST) Industry Usability Workshop.

- Finally, we have chosen the term *integrated* to distinguish our approach from the more generic approaches to UCD. Our approach emphasizes integration on several fronts:

  - Process—the approach has a logical sequence that relies on methods that fit together to generate data and design solutions. Further, it is integrated into an overall development process.

  - Team—the approach relies on a tightly knit group of multidisciplinary professionals.

  - Product—UCD produces an integrated total customer experience.

What Are the Benefits of Integrated UCD?

The major benefit of carrying out our integrated UCD is that it works (IBM, 2000). Companies can use it to develop products efficiently and with a high level of customer satisfaction.

The marketplace practices natural selection. People will naturally select the easiest way to do something — to find what they want, buy what they want, or do what they want. Complexity is the biggest inhibitor of product success. If customers find a product confusing or frustrating the first time they try to use it, they may not try it a second time. For this reason, usability is just as critical to business success as system availability, scalability, reliability, and functionality. Usability is vital to a company's success, its competitive edge, and perhaps even its survival. This is especially the case in the new world of Web-based or e-business applications. As companies make the transition to e-business, they have a unique opportunity to involve and impress those most important to the success of the business: their staff, their investors, and their clients. Well-designed applications are much more than a boon to corporate efficiency — they're a major asset to a company's reputation.

Ease of use may be invisible, but its absence certainly isn't invisible. Confusing, intimidating products make for confused, intimidated, and dissatisfied customers. And an unhappy customer becomes somebody else's customer. In an e-business world, the competition is not across the street or across a continent — it is a mouse-click away. Your e-business applications represent your company and your brand to users. In some cases, they're the *only* thing people have to identify you by. In an environment like this, you can't afford *not* to make ease of use a priority.

If usable design sounds like an expensive proposition, consider the alternative. The e-business marketplace is fast and fickle. Perception becomes reality. Product attributes become brand attributes. And poor product usability becomes a serious liability. Popular misperceptions at this stage of the game will cost you dearly. Damage can be done overnight — and it is not easily or quickly *undone*. For this reason, it's crucial that ease of use be integral to the product development process, and not an afterthought. Commercial success will go to those companies that make the commitment and investment necessary to ensure that usability is a hallmark of their business and e-business brand.

Before delving into the details of integrated UCD, we must point out that UCD is dramatically improving the ease of use of products, including software, hardware, and services. For example, the IBM workstation database product, DB2 Universal Database, used UCD starting with the 5.0 release. To enter new markets, expand market share, and increase profitability, IBM used UCD to raise the ease of use of the total customer experience with the product. The results of IBM's own studies, business results, and trade press reviews substantiate the improvement made in ease of use. For example, *PC Week* used the words "a vastly easier client setup procedure, integrated replication and a fresh new interface that's right on target." *InfoWorld* pointed out that the "Latest DB2 exceeds competition . . . administrative functions are well-integrated into the easy-to-use Control Center interface." *Information Week* wrote that "Installation, on both the server and client, is mind-numbingly easy . . . Universal Database is breathtaking for its enormous leap into ease of use."

UCD is also yielding significant benefits in the area of hardware. For example, the studies, business results, and trade press reviews for the IBM notebook computers ThinkPad 770 and 600 point to improvements made in ease of use. For example, *Gartner Report* wrote, "If winning in the notebook game is the result of attention to details, the 770 has it in spades, especially when it comes to usability." *PC Magazine* claimed, "The ThinkPad's [600] usability suffers no peer." *PC Computing* similarly echoed, "usability is where this machine truly shines." *Business Week* wrote, "IBM wins my vote for a huge display and excellent ergonomics. . . . The keyboard is the best I have ever seen in a laptop." *PC Week* similarly pointed out, "The Trackpoint is the most useful pointing device we've seen to date on a notebook." The business case derived from these types of results further drives the broad implementation of UCD at IBM.

What Types of Projects Can Benefit from the Approach?

UCD can apply to the design of any projects, from toasters to nuclear power plant control rooms and on to computer systems. However, the techniques described in this book have been optimized for information technology and other computer-related products.

Although UCD can be applied to all project categories, computer technology is the area that has the greatest opportunity for improvement in usability (Landauer, 1996). The explosion of the investment in computer technology by businesses and individuals has not led to a significant increase in productivity. Landauer and others concluded that the reason is because computers are simply too difficult to use. UCD, therefore, focuses on this important area of ease of use. Within the broad category of computers, UCD is relevant to hardware, software, and services. Further, it is just as applicable to the development of mass-market so-called commercial software as it is to one-of-a-kind custom, or "bespoke," system development that is done within a company. The terms *offering* and *product* are used interchangeably throughout this book, to include all these various types of projects for which UCD is relevant.

UCD has been applied to everything from high-end mainframe computers used to run the major corporations around the world to a multimedia encyclopedia used in the home and at school. It has also been used to design industry-leading notebook, desktop, and server computers as well as application development, database, networking, and productivity software. In the area of custom development, we've used UCD to design solutions in sectors such as the aircraft, healthcare, financial, insurance, and automotive industries. Recently, a prime focus has been on Web-based or e-business applications (Vredenburg et al., 1998).

What's the Primary Target of UCD?

Customer delight is the primary target of UCD. A key aspect of this delight involves usability. Usability is typically defined as

> *The extent to which a product can be used by specified users to achieve specified goals with effectiveness, efficiency and satisfaction in a specified context of use (ISO, 1999).*

Users determine the usability within a typical *context of use of the product*. In other words, the extent to which a product has the characteristic of usability is determined by the effectiveness of the product in allowing users to achieve their goals, the efficiency in carrying out their tasks, and the satisfaction the user experiences in interacting with the product. In our approach, usability is further broken down into subcomponents such as ease of acquisition, ease of installation, ease of learning, ease of use, ease of getting help, ease of getting support, and ease of removing the product.

To the user, usability is simply the quality of interaction with a product or system. In fact, most attributes of products such as capability, performance, reliability, installation, maintenance, documentation, and service are all correlated with usability. That is, when customers are asked in surveys to rate their satisfaction with any of these attributes, their ratings are highly influenced by their satisfaction with the product's usability.

CASE STUDY: THE IMPORTANCE OF USABILITY IN E-BUSINESS

- Business professionals identify usability as an important attribute of e-business applications.
- Surveys can be used to tap into the wants, needs, and opinions of the target audience.
- Automated survey tools can facilitate survey creation, administration, and data analysis.

To determine the relative importance of usability in the new and emerging area of e-business, the IBM Corporate UCD Team ran a study that yielded 142 responses from various business professionals. Respondents were asked to rate and rank various attributes of e-business applications. An e-business application was defined as follows:

> e-business applications improve business processes using
> Internet technologies. Examples of e-business applications
> include: communicating with other people via e-mail or
> groupware, Web site s where you can buy, sell, or complete
> other transactions, and connecting to corporate applications
> via the Web.

The study was conducted using the UCD Workbench tools, which will be described in Chapter 5. UCDSurvey was used to create a survey, post it to the Web, get responses, and then summarize the data. Figure 2.2 shows the survey.

The most interesting results of the survey concerned the importance of rankings. Respondents were asked to select the three most important e-business attributes. As shown in Figure 2.3, the item *usability* ranked 3 out of 10, both in terms of top priority and the weighted average of the top three priorities. The numbers in the table represent the number selecting each attribute. The weighted total was calculated as follows:

Priority	Point Assignment
First priority	1.0 point
Second priority	.66 points
Third priority	.33 points

These results show that security and reliability are the most important attributes to address on the Internet. However, it is critically important that usability came in third, right behind these major factors. In traditional product development, usability is often the most important attribute. In the e-business world, however, it is also

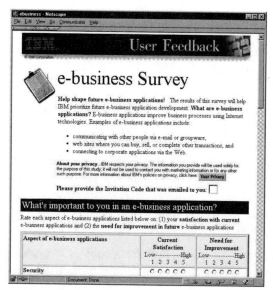

FIGURE 2.2

A user survey to determine the importance of usability in e-business. (Courtesy of IBM.)

Attribute	Importance Rank			
	First	**Second**	**Third**	**Weighted Total**
Security	70	14	13	83.5
Reliability	20	42	28	57.0
Usability	**14**	**18**	**26**	**34.5**
Speed	7	31	18	33.4
Capability	6	10	9	15.6
Integration	4	4	10	9.9
Customization	1	3	8	5.6
Administration	2	1	5	4.3
Engaging	1	1	2	2.3
Information and Assistance	0	1	3	1.7

FIGURE 2.3

Importance ranking for an e-business survey. (Courtesy of IBM.)

important, but security and reliability are added concerns that are sometimes seen as being more pressing.

The Six Principles of UCD

Making the transition from traditional design and development approaches to UCD usually involves a major cultural transformation for an organization and a paradigm shift for practitioners. To ensure success, companies typically need to take several steps to ensure that the key elements of this transition are carried out appropriately. These key steps include identifying core principles, carrying out education, and integrating UCD into the company's business and development process (Vredenburg, 1999). These elements, which are key to introducing UCD, will be discussed in Chapter 3.

For now, let's focus on the six core UCD principles that communicate the essence of UCD and serve as the framework for individual methods and techniques:

1. **Set business goals.** Determining the target market, intended users, and primary competition is central to all design and user participation.
2. **Understand users.** An understanding of the user is the driving force behind all design.
3. **Design the total customer experience.** Everything a customer sees, hears, and touches is designed together by a multidisciplinary team.
4. **Evaluate designs.** User feedback is gathered often with rigor and speed and drives product design.
5. **Assess competitiveness.** Competitive design requires a relentless focus on the ways users currently carry out the tasks and a determination to make designs add value.
6. **Manage for Users.** User feedback is integral to product plans, priorities, and decision making.

These principles are discussed in detail in the following sections.

Setting Business Goals

The first principle (Figure 2.4) involves determining the market segments to target, the customers and their characteristics within these segments, and the solution the majority of customers within the segment use today, that is, the competition for the offering. UCD must fit into a company's business strategy and demonstrably add financial value. It is critical to have this

UCD Principle #1

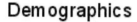

☑ **Set business goals**

Determining the target market, intended users, and primary competition is central to all design and user participation

Demographics

Purchasing habits

Competitors

FIGURE 2.4
Set business goals.

information in place at the start of a project. If this information does not exist or is incomplete, the rest of the User-Centered Design activities will be suspect.

Understanding Users

The second principle of UCD (Figure 2.5) says that an understanding of the user is the driving force behind all design. This principle is the basis of UCD. Without an appropriate focus on the way customers do things today and the way they want to do things differently in the future, design has no foundation.

To understand customers, UCD teams must understand their current and future tasks, the tools they employ to carry out the tasks, what problems they are experiencing with the tools, and the key characteristics of the environment in which they carry out their tasks (e.g., do they primarily work in groups or on the road).

UCD Principle #2

☑ **Understand Users**

**An understanding of the user is the
driving force behind all design**

Tasks

Tools Problems

Environment

FIGURE 2.5
Understand users.

CASE STUDY: UNDERSTANDING CUSTOMERS

- Understanding all segments of the target user audience is an essential step in UCD.
- Sharing target user profile information and keeping it at the front of everyone's minds help ensure that the design is truly user centered.
- Contacts from within a company are essential to supplying target user definition information.

A team consisting of user interaction designers, programmers, a user assistance designer, and content specialists used UCD on a project at MetLife to enhance and design a new graphical user interface for an existing claims processing system. The target audience for this new system consisted of users with many different job roles. For example, clerks would enter data into the system but would have no responsibility for claims processing. At the other end of the spectrum, case managers would have the authority to adjudicate claims. Other segments consisted of specialists such as vocational rehabilitation specialists and disability nurse specialists.

Some of these users would be allowed access to the system to input new or update existing claims, while others would be allowed only to view existing claims. Such a diverse target audience posed a design challenge: How do you optimize a system to meet the needs of all these user groups?

To provide a better design for this diverse audience, the team spent time on clearly identifying each of the user segments and the tasks performed. We created a large matrix of job roles and tasks. (See Table 2.1.) We distributed this matrix by posting it into our design notebook, a database containing all artifacts of the evolving design, user feedback data, and other materials needed by the team. We then summarized these data by collapsing the many audience segments into four main user groups. We copied this summary matrix onto a large poster board and posted it onto the walls of our work area as a constant reminder of the audience we were designing for. We used these data to help us set system security, that is, which users could access various parts of the system. We also used the data to decide which tasks to support "up front" in the user interface as opposed to those tasks that could be buried somewhat deeper within the interface. These data were also useful for creating testing scenarios for the various user segments.

This experience pointed out the importance of having a multidisciplinary design team of specialists from both outside and within an organization. It would be extremely difficult and time consuming for a consulting team consisting solely of design specialists from outside a company to understand the various job roles and responsibilities well enough to design a system to meet the needs of all its users.

TABLE 2.1
Selection from a user profile matrix.

Role	User Group	Unit	Tasks
• Unit Manager (n = 53) •Directors (n = 10)	A	Claims	• Inquire on claim for various info. • Review and approve payments over case manager's authority • Inquire on Work Queues to determine workload and backlog • Update Claim Diary to document phone calls, action plans, etc. •Update Claim data items on occasion

TABLE 2.1
Selection from a user profile matrix. (cont.)

Role	User Group	Unit	Tasks
• Disability Nurse Specialist (n=45) • Medical Consultant (n=20)	B	Claims	• Scan through Claim Diary entries to locate those concerning medical diagnosis, treatment, prognosis • Read selected Claim Diary entries to become familiar with claimant's clinical situation • Review Treatment Screen information for diagnosis codes, treatment dates, physician phone number, Claim End Date • Create Claim Diary entries summarizing clinical information, phone conversations, recommendations to case manager

Designing the Total Customer Experience

The third principle of UCD (Figure 2.6) focuses on the design of the total customer experience and says that everything a customer sees, hears, and touches is designed together by a multidisciplinary team. A critical ingredient of UCD is that the design effort must focus on the total solution and all aspects of the customer experience. That is, it should be

- Easy to buy
- Easy to set up
- Easy to learn
- Easy to use
- Intuitive
- Engaging
- Useful

You might be wondering why buying is considered part of the focus of UCD. Well, things like advertising and packaging typically lead to the first customer experience with an offering. They set up expectations, establish a design signature, and yield the first positive or negative reaction to the offering. If they set an unrealistic expectation, establish a poor or inconsistent design signature, or yield a negative first impression for the offering, the success of the design of the actual product is compromised before anyone even touches it.

You might also be wondering about the attributes *intuitive* and *engaging*. There was a time when *usable* meant the absence of obvious user problems.

UCD Principle #3

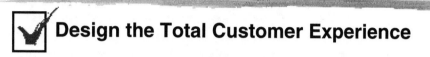

✓ Design the Total Customer Experience

Everything a customer sees and touches is designed together by a multidisciplinary team

Easy to Buy

Useful

Engaging   Easy to Set Up

Intuitive   Easy to Learn

Easy to Use

FIGURE 2.6
Design the total customer experience.

However, the competitive bar has been raised to the point where products now must be able to accommodate easily what users want to do and to provide a design that is pleasing and enjoyable. (Jordan, 2000)

All these criteria reinforce the need to design the total customer experience with specialists from various disciplines.

CASE STUDY: DESIGNING THE TOTAL CUSTOMER EXPERIENCE

- Design all aspects of the system with the characteristics of the target audience in mind.
- Pay particular attention to giving users a positive "out-of-the-box experience."
- Whenever possible, turn negative aspects of the system design into opportunities for delight.

The IBM RS/6000 desktop and deskside systems were designed to be consistent, user friendly, and appealing to their intended users. The target user audience for these products was system administrators, who could best be described at the time of this work to be young professionals who live and breathe computers. The packaging was designed to smoothly orchestrate the hardware set up and software installation through carefully presented, sequenced materials, and was based on usability studies of the tasks required for a successful set up. This logical ordering of materials avoided the "Christmas effect," where users scatter packaging and components around the room, digging for (and sometimes even discarding) items needed at various stages of the setup. Collateral material was included to capture the customers' interest and enthusiasm for the system. Users opened the product box to find a t-shirt, a mouse pad, a copy of *Wired* magazine, and games that showcased the 3D graphics capabilities of the system such as Quake (see Figure 2.7). This approach to design worked beautifully. It became cool to have an RS/6000. One of the most common questions asked by customers in the feedback survey was "Where can I get another t-shirt?" One customer manager reported having to hold a raffle to give away the t-shirts because users who had been assigned systems from other vendors were jealous.

Additional efforts were made to ensure that the users' experience with the system would be positive from the very beginning. In one case, usability testing found that users were impatient the first time they booted the system because it went through a lengthy initial configuration process. The product designers decided to include a bag of microwave popcorn with the computer. When the system reached the configuration step, the instructions suggested the user enjoy some popcorn. Later, the installation process was changed to minimize the configuration delay.

Evaluating Designs

The principle of evaluating designs (Figure 2.8) focuses on gathering user feedback to the evolving design and says that user feedback is gathered often, with rigor and speed, and drives product design.

Feedback must be frequent to be useful. Effective UCD teams schedule a feedback session once a week or once every two weeks. That way, when issues come up on the team like "I think customers would want it this way or that," the team can save the time they would spend arguing and simply get input on it at the next scheduled session. Rigor is also important. Simply asking a customer or two what they think is not sufficient. This type of approach can be misleading. There may be problems with bias, lack of

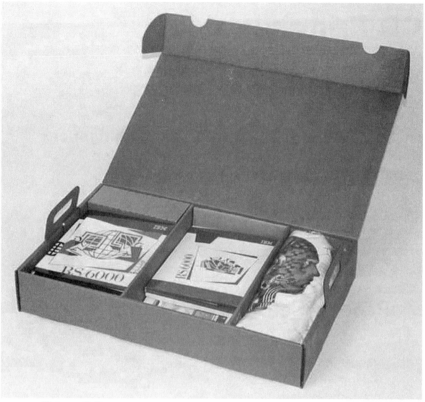

FIGURE 2.7
Boxes designed to organize materials and prevent shifting in transit. (Courtesy of IBM.)

objectivity, and lack of thoroughness. Instead, UCD specifies particular user feedback methods that can ensure that user feedback is gathered with rigor.

Finally, the feedback collected from users must drive product design, or it makes no sense to collect the feedback at all. There are two basic approaches to collecting feedback on design. The first is typically referred to as "low-fi" prototyping, which involves getting feedback using paper-and-pencil mockups of designs. This method is most appropriate early in a design cycle and is preferable even when higher fidelity prototypes are available. Users give better input when it is clear to them that the design is not "finished" and that their input can actually be accommodated. The second type of feedback requires hands-on design validation testing of a working prototype or actual early product.

UCD Principle #4

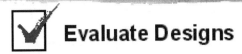

☑ **Evaluate Designs**

User feedback is gathered often with rigor and speed and drives product design

Paper & Pencil

Hands-on

FIGURE 2.8
Evaluate designs.

Several methods for gathering user feedback at various stages of UCD will be discussed in Chapter 5.

CASE STUDY: EVALUATING DESIGN

- Formal usability lab testing is an excellent way to evaluate mature designs.
- Multidisciplinary collaboration in usability testing can enhance the testing.
- Usability labs can facilitate collaborative test administration.

Formal usability lab testing is an excellent tool for the thorough evaluation of designs that have matured into high-fidelity prototypes or to actual program code. One example of a usability test performed by our team was a usability test of an application that enables computer salespeople to configure large mainframe systems. Multidisciplinary involvement in the testing made this test particularly effective. Throughout the entire test, the user research specialist sat beside the design team leader. The latter was one of two human-computer interaction (HCI) designers for this application. He had a thorough understanding of the context in which the application was to be used. He knew his users. He was therefore able to expand upon the questions and observations of the user feedback specialist, help interpret users' behaviors, and help elicit more detailed comments from the participants, all in real time. Because the test was performed in a usability lab (Figure 2.9), the participants were not privy to those discussions; the collaboration didn't interfere with the test. The result was a test and, ultimately, an application that benefited greatly from this multidisciplinary collaboration.

Assessing competitiveness

The fifth UCD principle (Figure 2.10) concerns assessing competitiveness and says that competitive design requires a relentless focus on the competition and its customers.

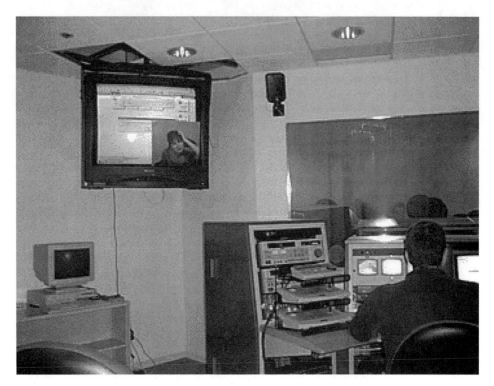

FIGURE 2.9
A composite video frame from a usability test lab. (Courtesy of IBM.)

UCD Principle #5

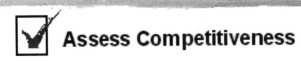 **Assess Competitiveness**

**Competitive design requires a relentless focus
on the competition and its customers**

Understand
Use

Evaluate
Solutions

Test
Head-to-Head

FIGURE 2.10
Assess competitiveness.

What we mean by *competitor* here is whatever the majority of customers are using today to carry out the tasks. The competition may be an actual competitor company's product, a combination of products, or even some analog (nontechnology) methods.

Scott Cook, the CEO of Intuit Corporation, maker of Quicken, the popular financial tool, often talks about how he is having difficulty unseating his main competitor. He talks about how tough this competitor is and how pervasive it is in the market. At this point, everyone thinks he is referring to Microsoft, but he isn't. He points out that his main competitor is the pen. It has total portability, ease of use, and a tough-to-beat price point. However, he says that he feels that as long as he focuses his company on this competitor, in addition to Microsoft, of course, then it will be positioned for continued leadership.

Development organizations and companies commonly feel that their product is unique and that it doesn't have any competitors. As Scott Cook's position shows, virtually all products have some sort of competitor, some way people manage to do tasks without your product. This is the way we need to view competitors in terms of UCD. We must examine our competitors by understanding the use of their offerings, evaluate our solutions relative to theirs, and carry out head-to-head, task-based user tests to compare our solutions to theirs.

CASE STUDY: ASSESSING COMPETITIVENESS

- It's important to identify all your competitors.
- You can use photographs and videos to capture competitors' designs.
- You should share your data with all interested parties.

On a recent project to design a kiosk for a large automobile manufacturer, an evaluation of the competition was one of the first activities performed. A user research specialist from the UCD team examined two sets of competitors. First, she looked at existing automotive kiosks. Fortunately, a wealth of these kiosks existed all in one place: the annual Detroit Auto Show. (See Figure 2.11.)

The second set of competitors, the team reasoned, would be best-of-breed kiosks in general. (See Figure 2.12.) Again, the team sought a place where a large number of kiosks existed all in one location. The team found this at EPCOT Center. The user research specialist designed a heuristic evaluation checklist. She examined kiosks that attracted many users, as well as those that stood idle. She noted design strengths and weaknesses. She took photographs and videos and brought them back to the development team. She then presented the data at a large meeting of everyone involved with the project. She wrote and distributed a report containing the photos.

Managing for Users

The last and perhaps most important UCD principle (Figure 2.13) concerns managing for users and says that user feedback is integral to product plans, priorities, and decision making. An organization can be completely in alignment with the first five principles, but if it's not in alignment with this one, all is lost. There have been projects that had highly motivated design teams doing wonderful design based on user input, but the design never got integrated into the product; in turn, users didn't realize the benefits of the work.

Building ease of use into offerings using UCD involves a set of business decisions. As with everything else, therefore, ease of use needs to be managed into offerings, starting with making the appropriate investment decisions, setting ease of use objectives, building appropriate resources into the development/production plan, acquiring the requisite key skills, tracking and fixing user problems found through customer feedback sessions, and

FIGURE 2.11
An automotive kiosk.

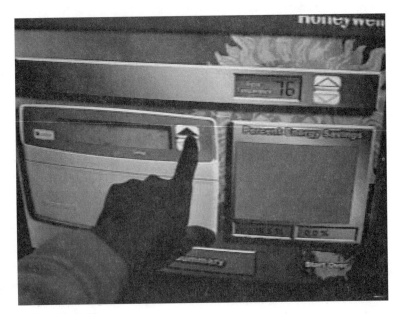

FIGURE 2.12
A screen from a well-designed kiosk.

UCD Principle #6

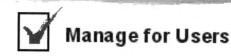

☑ Manage for Users

User feedback is integral to product plans, priorities, and decision making

Investment

EOU Objectives   Resources

Skills   User Problems

Results

FIGURE 2.13
Manage for users.

keeping focused on the results from a customer perspective by tracking customer satisfaction.

Multidisciplinary Design and User Feedback _____

Two fundamental elements of a successful implementation of UCD are multidisciplinary design and user feedback.

Multidisciplinary Design Specialists

UCD requires that specialists from several disciplines create the total customer experience. These roles can be organized into a conceptual team structure, which includes individuals who *design*, those who are *architects*, those who provide *information*, and those who *lead*. (See Figure 2.14.) The work of all these individuals is informed by guidelines, processes, and tools, as well as by customer input and user evaluation. Even though all these categories of roles come together and synergistically create the total customer experience, it is important to point out the differences in the contributions made by each.

The customer directly experiences the results of design. Architecture specifies a framework, flow, or assembly that is the context for design. Design and architecture both rely heavily on a variety of information, including specification of the target market, customer audience, requirements, user tasks, and competitor strengths and weaknesses, all of which are gathered via customer input. The design is then evaluated by users. Leadership is required to set the vision and direction for the project in terms of achieving a particular total customer experience, to manage the deliverables and plans, and to lead the multidisciplinary team. Finally, the work of the individuals on the team is influenced by guidelines, processes, and tools to ensure that a consistent design signature exists across products, that activities are carried out according to best practices, and that tools appropriate to the task are used.

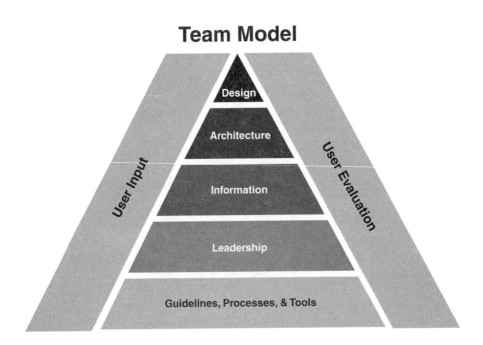

FIGURE 2.14
The UCD team model. (Courtesy of IBM.)

CASE STUDY: MULTIDISCIPLINARY TEAMS

- All key skills must be represented on a UCD team.
- Team members must be able to understand one another, but not duplicate the skills of one another.
- Proximity is a powerful design aid.

Multidisciplinary teamwork was used on a recent project to develop an intranet site for a well-known automobile manufacturer. The team consisted of a network architect, a programming architect, a human-computer interaction designer, a visual designer, a Java programmer, a Lotus Domino programmer, and a project manager. All the skills needed to design the site were represented on this team. Team members overlapped in their expertise enough to communicate and work together effectively; however, each team member had a unique set of skills. Most of the team sat together in a single large cubicle. The quarters were tight, but the effect was extremely positive. Everyone was always aware of what everyone else was doing. Communication was ongoing and immediate. The design benefited from the input of all key players.

Although specific terminology for the roles on a UCD team might differ from company to company, specification of roles, responsibilities, and skills should address the various elements of this conceptual structure. The roles will be also discussed in the context of these conceptual categories.

Table 2.2 shows some of the terms commonly used to refer to the various roles on a UCD team.

TABLE 2.2
UCD Team member roles and titles.

UCD Role	Terminology
User experience design lead	Program manager, design lead, creative integrator, creative lead, creative director, ease of use lead, user experience design lead
Marketing specialist	Product manager, marketing, packaging engineer
Visual/industrial designer	Industrial design, mechanical design, graphics designer, media designer, artist, visual interface architect, mechanical engineer, director
Human-computer interaction designer	User interaction design, user interface design, interaction designer, designer, product designer, HCI designer, HCI specialist, information architect

TABLE 2.2
UCD Team member roles and titles. (cont.)

UCD Role	Terminology
User assistance architect	User communication design, user assistance designer, user assistance architect, writer, information designer
Technology architect	Programmer, technologist, architect, software designer, UI programmer
Service and support specialist	User support specialist, service planner, service and support engineer
User research specialist	Usability specialist, usability engineer, human factors engineer, user experience specialist, user experience architect, user research specialist, user feedback specialist
Internationalization/terminology specialist	Localization designer
UCD project lead	Program manager, project manager, product manager

In addition to the design team members, UCD is enabled by domain experts: specialists who are familiar with the content matter addressed by the product. In some cases, many of the team members may have domain-specific knowledge. In other cases, however, domain experts may need to be recruited to advise the team.

Design.   Although a number of individuals and disciplines contribute to design, the actual composition and rendering of the deliverable that customers will see, hear, and touch is done by the visual/industrial designer and the human-computer interaction designer. These specialists create the experience for the customer based on contributions from the other disciplines. The visual design includes the marketing materials, packaging, books, and installation, as well as the actual product user interface. In the case of software, the term *visual designer* is usually used, whereas in hardware, the term *industrial designer* is typically used. As shown in Table 2.2, other terms for this role include media designer, artist, and graphics designer. The human-computer interaction designer translates user tasks and task flow into an interaction design that satisfies user needs and wants while also providing the most efficient method of carrying out users' tasks.

Architecture.   The design of the total customer experience must be based on solid architecture. It is generally acknowledged that technology architecture is required, but it is often not realized that user assistance architecture is also critical as well. In the same vein, the technology architect needs to ensure that the computer system itself will be able to carry out the requirements of the design, and the user assistance architect needs to structure the information provided with the product to ensure that users will be able to learn to use the product and be able to get help using it in the most desirable way.

Information.   A number of roles are in place primarily to provide information to the design and architecture effort. Marketing specialists provide information regarding the target market, user audience, primary competitor, ease of use market objectives and messages, and channel and packaging requirements. Relevant market intelligence and other market research findings are also the responsibility of the marketing specialist. Customer service and support specialists provide information to the team and communicate requirements back to the service and support team. Internationalization and terminology specialists also provide information to the team. The user research specialist also has an information-providing role, planning, scheduling, conducting, analyzing, and interpreting the user feedback activities.

Leadership.   UCD team leadership is critically important. The UCD project lead provides leadership in terms of maintaining schedules, establishing dependencies, and keeping the project on track. The user experience design lead has the vision for the project, leads the multidisciplinary design team, and is the conscience of the team.

Team Member Responsibilities and Skills.   Responsibilities and skills associated with each of the UCD team member roles are outlined in Table 2.3. It is useful to remember that these are roles, rather than individuals. It would be a luxury for a team to have a one-to-one correspondence of role-to-person. However, in most cases, organizations do not have that many specialists that can be assigned to any single product team. An organization is more likely to have multiple roles assigned to a given team member. For example, the HCI designer may also need to perform the duties of user research specialist. Another example is for the UCD project lead to also be the user experience design lead. In this way, UCD can be scaled to meet the needs of a smaller project.

TABLE 2.3
UCD team responsibilities and skills.

Role	Responsibility	Skills
UCD project lead	Has overall responsibility for UCD deliverables and plans as well as the integration of them into the development plan	Project management, UCD process, development process
User experience design lead	Has responsibility for the total customer experience design of the project	Vision, leadership, technical expertise, project and people management, facilitation
Visual designer	Has responsibility for the overall appearance, layout, balance of the software offering including the consistent visual signature of the advertising, packaging, and product design	Art, design, model/ prototype building, creativity, teamwork
Industrial designer	Has responsibility for the overall appearance, layout, balance of the hardware offering including the consistent visual signature of the advertising, packaging, and product design	Art, design, model building, creativity, teamwork
HCI designer	Responsible for specifying the task flow, interaction design, and division of tasks to be carried out by the user and by the computer	Human-computer interaction, conceptual modeling, information synthesis
User assistance architect	Has responsibility to specify the appropriate user assistance mechanisms for the offering	Information architecture, teamwork
Technology architect	Has responsibility for specifying the underlying technology required to implement the desired total customer experience	Technical skill in relevant domain, development process, programming and/or engineering teamwork

TABLE 2.3
UCD team responsibilities and skills. (cont.)

Role	Responsibility	Skills
Marketing specialist	Specifies the target market, user audience, key competitor, market ease of use objectives, and ease of use messages as well as the channel, packaging, and terms and condition requirements	Marketing, market intelligence, market trends, synthesis of information, teamwork
Service and support specialist	Specifies the service and support that should be delivered with the offering	Service and support technologies and options
Internationalization and terminology specialist	Is responsible for ensuring that the offering appropriately addresses the needs of the international audience within the target market and for specifying the appropriate terminology to be used in the offering	Internationalization and localization specialization, terminology, languages, HL enablement
User research specialist	Has responsibility for the design, analysis, and interpretation of UCD studies carried out on the project including the articulation of recommendations coming from this applied research	Usability engineering, technical aptitude, UCD methods

User Feedback Methods

UCD typically involves a number of methods that require a range of low to high resource requirements, with many of the low-resource methods involving Internet-based surveys and remote user collaboration. The choice of which methods to use can vary widely across projects. However, UCD is best illustrated if we take one path through the various steps involved. The path described here is characterized by a medium level of required resource.

The cycle starts with an understanding of the customer audience the offering is targeted at and proceeds to an assessment of the competitor's design. It is followed first by a high-level design of the offering and an evaluation of it, and then a lower-level iterative design with user evaluation and validation. Early-ship user feedback and a head-to-head hands-on comparison test complete the multidisciplinary design of the total customer experience. (See Figure 2.15.)

Each of the activities in the UCD cycle is described in more detail in Chapter 4.

Project Optimization

Integrated UCD focuses heavily on various strategies for optimizing deployment. It uses technology to move from a largely manual process to one that is much more automated and efficient. The various approaches are discussed in detail in Chapter 5. The case study in this section gives you an idea of what kind of optimization we're talking about. The example looks at three elements of carrying out UCD: getting candidate participants, carrying out a study, and analyzing results (see Figures 2.16 and 2.17). Ways of using the Internet and intranet to optimize these various elements will be shown.

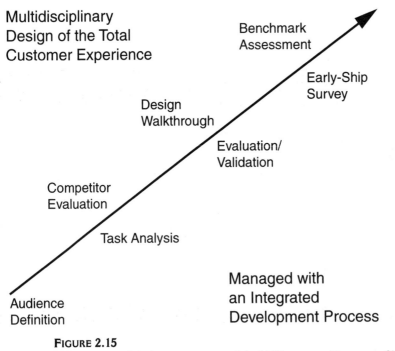

FIGURE 2.15
An illustration of the key components of the UCD process. (Courtesy of IBM.)

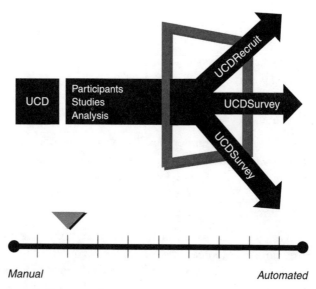

FIGURE 2.16
UCD can be optimized with tools that automate the process of recruiting, conducting studies, and carrying out data analysis.

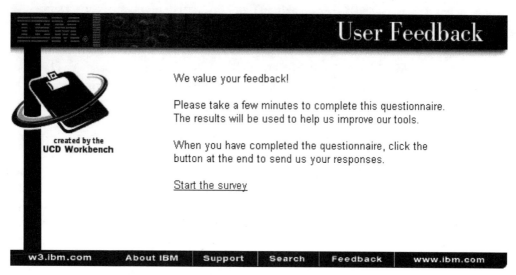

FIGURE 2.17
Desktop online survey to assess key attributes of operating system use. (Courtesy of IBM.)

CASE STUDY: OPTIMIZING UCD

- Time and resource limitations can be overcome by using automated user feedback gathering tools.
- Survey data can yield new information, validate known information, and dispel widely held beliefs about user behavior.
- Using the Internet to gather user feedback gives a team access to an international sample of users.

A team at IBM needed information rapidly on the way users interacted with the Microsoft Windows operating system. The team wanted to know such things as how many windows users typically had open at the same time, how they normally started programs, how they switched between programs, and whether they ordinarily ran programs maximized or with multiple windows showing on the desktop.

However, the team was on a very tight development schedule and decided that it didn't have the time or resources to conduct the required study. It was suggested that the team consider using a Web survey. The team decided to follow the suggestion. The survey was constructed, the participants were selected and invited, and the data was collected, analyzed, and presented back to the team—all within three days. The results yielded important insights for the team (Figure 2.18). It learned that the majority of the participants do not change settings on the interface from the defaults and that little use was made of advanced features. For example, the majority left the task bar at the bottom of the screen with auto-hide turned off. Results also showed that despite having higher resolution monitors, a large number of participants maximized windows and switched between them using the task bar.

Results like these had a major impact on subsequent design direction. Comments from teams who have used this approach have been extremely positive. They realize that the use of mechanisms like these for rapidly collecting input from representative customers not only increases the knowledge they have of their users but it also allows them to collect this information when they don't have the time to use traditional methods. The input is also from an international sample. Despite their speed and power, the team knew that these methods should not be used as a replacement for all of the typical UCD methods and techniques. The team knew that it should augment the traditional methods in critical projects when there is extreme time pressure, a larger sample is desired, or a worldwide audience is important. In circumstances in which a project would normally get no customer input, these mechanisms can be used to ensure that some customer input is collected.

Despite the speed and power of these low-resource methods, it should be pointed out that they should not replace the traditional UCD methods and techniques. They should augment the traditional methods in critical

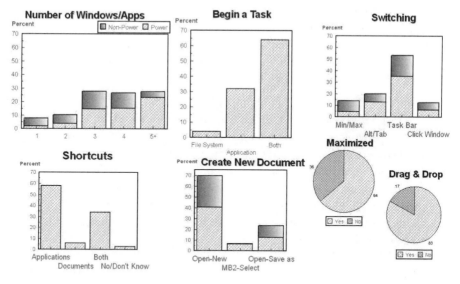

FIGURE 2.18

Summary of study results showing the typical number of open windows, ways of beginning a task, method of switching windows, types of shortcuts used, and method of creating a new document as well as the percent who use windows maximized and the drag-and-drop technique.

projects, in cases where there is extreme time pressure, where a larger sample is desired, and where a worldwide audience is important. In certain circumstances where a project would normally get no user input, these mechanisms can be used to ensure that some user input is collected.

CASE STUDY: USING INTERNET-BASED USER EVALUATION METHODS

- The Internet affords easy access to a large and diverse group of representative customers.
- Iterative design can be done over the Internet using surveys, bitmapped low-fidelity prototypes, high-fidelity executable code and Web-based prototypes, and other tools.
- UCD activities can be modified to exploit the medium of the Internet.

The Internet offers a tremendous opportunity to reach a wide variety of representative users for input to various UCD activities. UCD methods were used in the design of the conference registration Web site for the Usability Professionals' Association. Volunteers were solicited by posting a notice to a popular forum for usability professionals. A note was sent to all volunteers explaining that they would be participating in the design of the Web site. Then, a few volunteers were selected for each of the activities. Task analysis was performed by sending participants a list of tasks and asking them to rate the tasks and to add missing tasks. The conceptual model was evaluated by having users review text and drawings of task groupings and flow. These were translated into hand-sketched, low-fidelity prototypes. (See Figures 2.19–2.21.) High-fidelity prototypes were evaluated via the Web. (See Figure 2.22.) All these activities involved iterations of design based on user feedback.

The respondents for this design effort were admittedly a unique group of users. They were capable of wearing two hats: user and usability expert. Having such a population to work with made many aspects of UCD easier. For example, when designing the site architecture, it was not necessary to explain the affinity grouping method we used. Other groups of participants might need more instructions for participating in remote studies. Phone calls, Web chats, and other tools such as whiteboards and video could be used to help explain and implement the UCD methods. (See Chapter 5.)

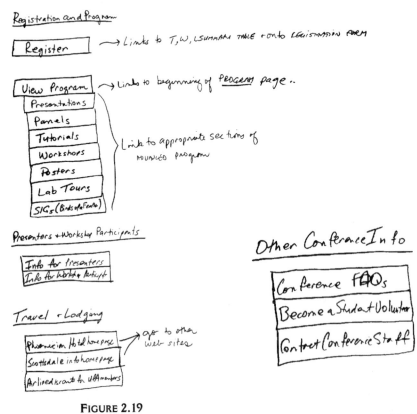

FIGURE 2.19
Low-fidelity prototype of Web site navigation bar. (Courtesy of the Usability Professionals' Association.)

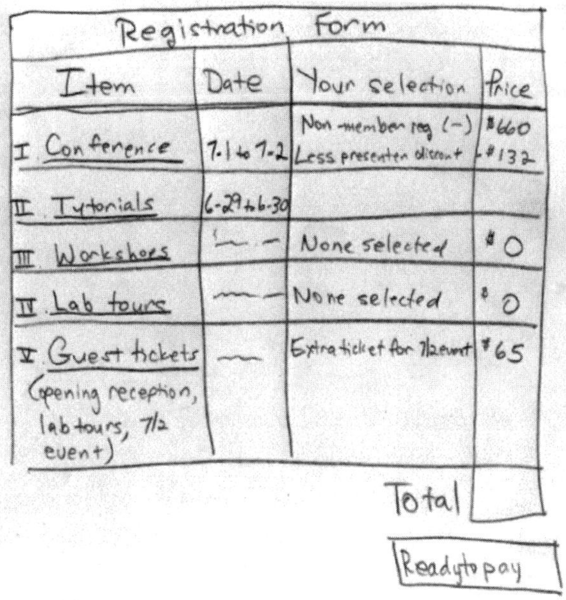

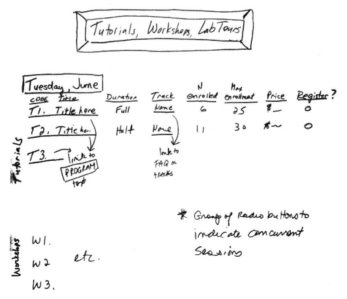

FIGURE 2.20
Low-fidelity prototype of registration form. (Courtesy of the Usability Professionals' Association.)

FIGURE 2.21
Low-fidelity prototype of tutorial page. (Courtesy of the Usability Professionals' Association.)

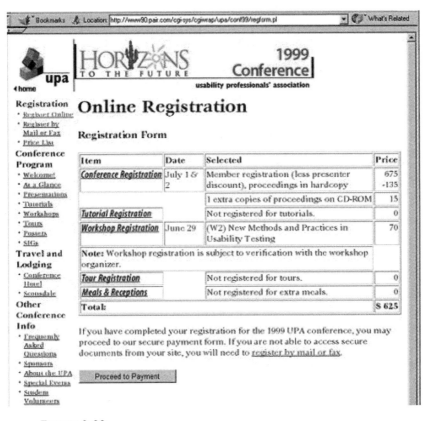

FIGURE 2.22
High-fidelity prototype. (Courtesy of the Usability Professionals' Association.)

Providing Universal Access with UCD

UCD is all about designing products that best suit customers. One critically important element of accomplishing this goal concerns designing for all members of a target market and not just those who reside in the United States and who have good vision and are otherwise healthy. The majority of information technology products are developed in the United States, whereas the majority of customers in most markets reside outside the United States. Most computer products assume excellent vision, even though many users don't have this, and with an increasingly aging population, this situation will get worse. Individuals with other physical characteristics that influence their use of computer technology should also be addressed. Currently, the World Wide Web Consortium (W3C) provides guidance for designing for accessibility. Additionally, in the United States, section 508 of the Rehabilitation Act Amendments of 1998 requires that all information technology products used or developed by the federal government be accessible to employees with disabilities. Similar policies have been or are currently being enacted in many countries.

As discussed further in Chapter 5, the selection of participants in UCD studies and the method of contacting them needs to take into account these "universal access" considerations. Not doing so will exacerbate an already less than optimal situation with products not appropriately designed for all users in a target market. Focusing on universal access, however, also provides a great business opportunity, especially given the direction of e-business applications, which by their very nature are worldwide in their availability but can also be made accessible to all potential users with the right design.

CASE STUDY: DESIGNING FOR UNIVERSAL ACCESS

- It is important that user feedback study participants be representative of the target audience.
- UCD activities can be modified to accommodate participants with special needs such as those with visual impairments.
- Often, low-tech methods can be easier to modify to accommodate participants with special needs than high-tech methods can.

Designers often attempt to accommodate users with visual impairments by allowing users to control various settings such as font size. In some cases, however, a product may be designed specifically for a visually impaired target audience. Such was the case for a point-of-sale system for the visually impaired. A user research specialist colleague of ours participated in a task analysis session intended to gather tasks and requirements for the development of this system. Members of the design team and representative customers who were, by definition, visually impaired, participated in the session. During the session, activities that are usually employed during task analysis were modified to accommodate the visually impaired participants. For example, as in most task flow modeling exercises, tasks were written on sticky notes and posted onto walls. Participants organized these tasks by moving the sticky notes into groups. However, in this particular session, tasks were written in large, bold text, and were reread aloud frequently to help participants better manipulate them.

This session used an effective, low-tech method for gathering tasks. However, it would also be possible to gather tasks from visually impaired users using a decision support center (DSC). A DSC is an electronic meeting room. (See Figure 2.23.) Several PCs in a LAN configuration serve as workstations for meeting participants. Group collaboration software runs on the PCs. When gathering data from visually impaired users, large monitors running this software at a low resolution with a screen magnification utility are available to enhance participants' ability to participate. For more completely visually impaired participants, screen-reader programs are required. In such cases, more text-oriented software is preferable to GUIs. In such cases, reverting to older, DOS-based versions of groupware programs might be beneficial. In any case, it is critical that actual representative customers for such systems be accommodated.

FIGURE 2.23
Decision support center used in the study. (Courtesy of IBM.)

Summary

In this chapter we discussed the ways in which the Integrated UCD approach is unique, what its key benefits are, the types of products for which UCD is appropriate, the derivation of the name, and the target of UCD—customer delight. We also explained the six core principles of UCD, discussed the multidisciplinary design element of UCD, examined the user feedback elements of UCD, and introduced project optimization of UCD and designing for univeral access. In Chapter 3 we'll explore ways to introduce UCD into an organization.

Introducing the Approach

3

Introducing the Approach _____

Information technology companies, by their very nature, are not typically fertile ground on which to sow the seeds of UCD. They are staffed by technologically savvy engineers who often have difficulty understanding the needs of the common person. Whereas other technology-based approaches to design and development may be more readily adopted in these companies, introducing a UCD approach requires special attention. Much of the knowledge contained in Chapter 2 has been available to experts in the field for a decade or two. Yet, very little of that knowledge has been used within organizations to date because the benefits of good usability and the costs of poor usability have only recently become widely recognized. Some companies have made dramatic differences by adopting and practicing UCD, but many have failed to appreciate the benefits of this approach to product design (Mao, Vredenburg, Smith, and Carey, 2001). The difficulty of getting these ideas adopted by organizations, therefore, requires some attention.

There are three fundamental differences in the integrated approach to UCD. First, the more comprehensive approach includes a focus on the total customer experience. Second, Integrated UCD focuses heavily on the factors that must be addressed when introducing it to a company. Third, efficiency and time-to-market concerns are addressed largely with the use of advanced technology. The first factor was addressed in Chapter 2, the second factor is the focus of the present chapter, and the third factor will be addressed in Chapter 5.

Our collective experience, and that of industry colleagues, suggests that the following factors are particularly effective strategies for introducing UCD to an organization. In most organizations, any one of the following may not be sufficient. Rather, a number of the factors carried out together will likely be the most successful approach.

Make the Message Simple

Think of the process of introducing UCD to an organization as being similar to advertising a product or to teaching a foreign language. In advertising, you only get one chance to make a first impression. The advertising profession is very aware of this and, as a result, makes marketing messages powerful yet simple. Similarly, anyone who has tried to teach a foreign language or tried to understand someone speaking in a foreign language also knows about the value of keeping the message simple. Given that introducing UCD to an organization requires advertising and involves teaching a new and foreign language (the language of UCD), simplicity in the message is critical.

The first messages about UCD should communicate the essence of the approach and its value. Formulating a set of core *UCD Principles* is a particularly effective way of doing this. However, to keep the audience focused, you should provide no more than a handful of principles. An example of a good set of principles follows (Vredenburg, 1999):

- **Set business goals.** Determining the target market, intended users, and primary competition is central to all design and user participation.
- **Understand users.** An understanding of the user is the driving force behind all design.
- **Design the total customer experience.** Everything a customer sees, hears, and touches is designed together by a multidisciplinary team.
- **Evaluate designs.** User feedback is gathered, often with rigor and speed, and drives product design.

- **Assess competitiveness.** Competitive design requires a relentless focus on the ways users currently carry out the tasks and makes designs add value.
- **Manage for users.** User feedback is integral to product plans, priorities, and decision making.

Make sure that the principles are appropriate for your organization. Having key decision makers within your organization brainstorm to come up with statements specific to an organization can be a good way to do this. This pursuit will ensure that you'll end up with relevant principles and will effectively get key members of your organization "on-board" and have them "bought in" by having them customize the introduction.

Making the message simple isn't just relevant to creating a set of core principles. It is also relevant to any communication that happens regarding UCD within your organization. For example, if you give a presentation on UCD to your organization, keep the set of presentation pages and their content short and simple. Often, specialists from core UCD fields such as human factors engineering will often try to communicate too many details. Even though a great level of detail may be appropriate when presenting a paper to peers at a professional conference, it is not appropriate for presenting UCD to senior management or development organizations.

Here are some other simple messages that can be used to focus attention on the need for UCD (IBM, 1999):

- Is your technology showing?
- Nobody buys ease of use. But nobody buys products without it either.
- Ease of use may be invisible, but its absence sure isn't.
- UCD—mastering the obvious.
- Want to make the most of the e-business opportunity? *Easy* does it.
- Do you know who your users are?
- Learn from experience—the *customers'*.
- Engineering the killer app isn't exactly child's play. But using it better be.

Even when UCD has been successfully introduced and deployment has started, it is still important to continue to keep the message simple. For example, when reporting status on progress, use two or three key metrics to indicate that progress is optimal.

UCD doesn't need to be complicated or take much time, money, or people; and the communication of UCD shouldn't give this impression. The material you use to introduce UCD must be powerful and simple. Many organizations try to introduce UCD with a weak or complex presentation and never get past the introduction.

Spend Time on Education

Together with a set of principles on which everyone can focus and other simple messages, you should also plan to educate the engineers in your company with anything from an overview presentation to a full-fledged set of classes.

When programmers are introduced to a new language, such as C++ or Java, managers are typically quick to see the value in sending them to classes to learn the new language. However, many managers and senior executives don't feel the same way about education and training in UCD. In fact, many believe that these skills can be "just picked up." Others believe that hiring one human factors specialist should give them everything they need. This one person should be able to do all the "UCD stuff"; if others need to know more they can simply pick it up from this specialist. This approach is often a recipe for failure. First, all members of the multidisciplinary team have key roles to play in carrying out UCD. Simply expecting one specialist to do the entire job misses the point of UCD. Second, it is impossible for any one person to do all that is required on most commercial projects. Third, much of the knowledge and skills involved cannot just be picked up. Fourth, you make the vote for UCD a vote of one. If there are any political issues for implementing UCD, you make all those issues the problems of one person even if "the right people" buy in initially. If that person tries to solve all the problems, he will become "the problem" or simply "trouble." It is possible to wait for the rest of the organization to "discover" the problems, but the time to a solution will be costly both for the company and the career of the UCD specialist.

So, what education is optimal? From our experience, four types of education and training are required—awareness, executive, introductory, and advanced. We describe each type in this section.

CASE STUDY: UCD EDUCATION

- Assume little or no prior knowledge about UCD.
- Design for both knowledge acquisition and emotional buy-in.
- Practice what you preach.

A group of IBM educators with a background in product development and human factors designed a one-day course to teach the basics of UCD. To make these courses relevant to the population for which it was being designed, requirements were gathered and validated, other courses were examined, and pilot versions were tested. In short, UCD was employed in course design. During this phase, the course developers found that, although many product designers and developers believed they already knew about UCD, they instead held many misconceptions and outdated concepts. The course was, therefore, constructed to introduce UCD as an alternative to traditional product development.

A guiding force in the design of this course was that raising the awareness of attendees to the importance of UCD to product design is as important as teaching about UCD tools and techniques. Role playing helps to increase awareness by involving students experientially. For example, during the design walkthrough module, students role-play as participants in the walkthrough, where they actually assess alternative designs.

To get buy-in from a highly technical audience, a course about UCD must employ current technologies and be aesthetically appealing. Multimedia files, such as movie clips, photographs, graphics, and sound bytes, are integrated into the slides to help illustrate concepts in an entertaining manner. Wall hangings, handouts, readings, and exercises must also be employed to reinforce the main messages. Figure 3.1 shows a sample slide from the course materials.

Awareness

The objective of this category of education is simple awareness of what UCD is and what value it has. Awareness education can take the form of a 15-to-60 minute introductory presentation given at a regularly scheduled, all-employee meeting of the organization. A sample presentation is included on the CD that accompanies this book. In large companies where a number of these types of meetings may be taking place, the preparation of a short video of this material may also be appropriate. Sample videos are also included on the CD. The videos can then be distributed from organization to organization, thereby minimizing the impact on those introducing the approach within the company. Awareness can also be accomplished in a variety of other ways to reinforce the key messages in these presentations.

Other examples of ways of increasing awareness include creating a logo or visual identifier for the approach and including that on such things as mugs, t-shirts, and mouse pads (see Figure 3.2). These inexpensive logo items can be given to members of your organization who have taken a UCD class, participated in a UCD user session, or provided a good suggestion for

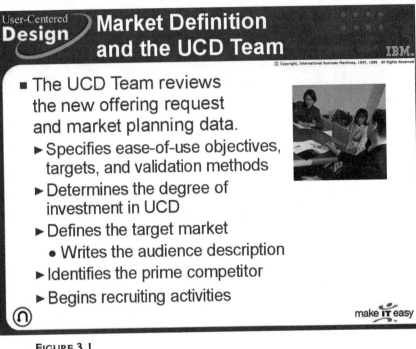

FIGURE 3.1
Slide from a UCD course. (Courtesy of IBM.)

FIGURE 3.2
UCD logos. (Courtesy of IBM.)

how to better implement UCD within your company. After a while, many people within your organization will recognize the logo and know what it means. Another idea that a number of organizations have used to increase awareness of UCD and ease of use in general involves organizing an open house or demo day. These events can be fairly simple but provide a great opportunity to show others the benefits of UCD. Early in deployment, when your organization doesn't have its own examples of UCD and ease of use success, other products from the industry that are known for their ease of use can be demonstrated. When your organization has examples of its own, teams that created the success can tell their peers about their experiences.

You may be saying to yourself that you don't need any of this awareness material and that you would like to go directly to the more substantive education and training material. Experience suggests that a focus on the awareness category of material, in addition to the material we're about to cover, is critically important in most organizations. The awareness material is the only education material that can get to everyone in your organization. The importance of having everyone in the company aware of UCD should not be underestimated.

Note, however, that the amount and type of material you choose to present depends on your audience. If you're in a company of five employees including the CEO, then you'll be able to streamline this material further. The objectives you have for the organization will also influence how much material you present. If, for example, you're just interested in getting a little more focus on the user within your organization, but really don't intend to make it something that your products will be known for, then you'll want to adopt a lighter weight approach (see Chapter 5 for ideas). On the other hand, if you want to increase dramatically the ease of use of your products, you'll want to adopt the full set of recommendations provided here.

CASE STUDY: COST-JUSTIFYING UCD

- Product managers and other development staff want proof that UCD works.

- Cost-justification analysis is one method that helps demonstrate the dollar value of UCD.

- It is easier to demonstrate the value of UCD over time and across projects if cost justification information is available.

One of the most challenging aspects of UCD is demonstrating that it works. Product managers and others involved in the development effort often challenge us to prove that the resources allocated to UCD are worth the expense. One of the strategies that have worked in the past is to demonstrate that UCD has led to cost savings. It is best to give an example that is close to home (i.e., a product developed by the audience members' own company). The best examples tend to involve a cost-justification analysis, as described in Bias and Mayhew (1994). Figures 3.3–3.6 show simple before-and-after screen grabs accompanied by UCD testing data and a cost-justification analysis of the amount of money saved through UCD.

Cost-justification analysis is most effective when productivity is one of the main product goals. But such an analysis can also be applied when a product has other goals (e.g., marketplace presence). In all cases, it is important to have a UCD team identify the product goals during the early phases of UCD so that the attainment of these goals can be assessed when the product is released.

The difficulty in demonstrating the value of usability lies in tying attainment of the goals to the UCD effort. We have found that any single successful UCD effort does not offer enough "proof" to make the case for UCD. Rather, what does seem effective is showing that as UCD permeates an organization, the overall quality of products with regard to meeting user wants and needs improves. This corroboration requires both time for the UCD process to gain momentum and careful tracking of UCD efforts and their results.

The following figures depict an interface before and after applying UCD principles, test results, and cost savings.

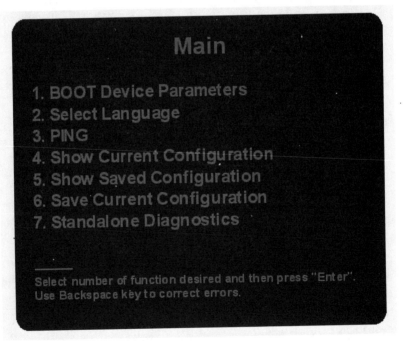

FIGURE 3.3
The original screen.

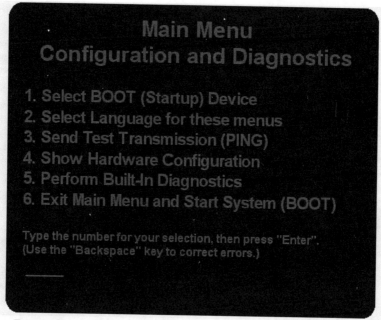

FIGURE 3.4
The revised screen.

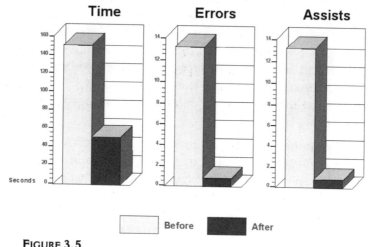

FIGURE 3.5
UCD test results.

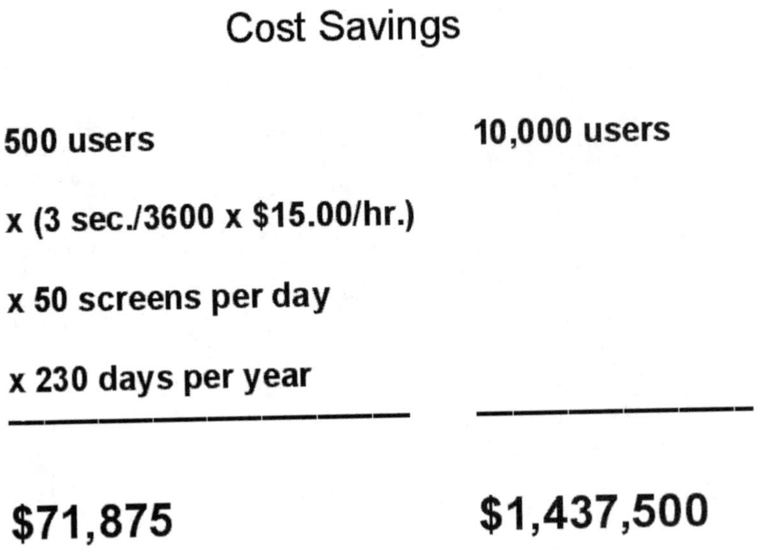

Cost Savings

500 users   **10,000 users**

x (3 sec./3600 x $15.00/hr.)

x 50 screens per day

x 230 days per year
_____   _____

$71,875   **$1,437,500**

FIGURE 3.6
Cost savings.

Executive

Education for executives may not seem to be important. After all, executives are usually not the members of the organization who design the products. However, they do make the product strategy decisions and the resource allocations. They also often set the vision and determine what the organization will see as important. It will be easier to institute a successful UCD program if you have executive support. For these reasons, it is very important to ensure that your executive team is aware of the key concepts of UCD and know what they need to do differently to manage within an organization that is using UCD.

Even though you may think that the awareness material discussed in the previous section would be perfectly appropriate for executives, this typically isn't the case. Our experience shows that a different approach is required for executives. The approach that has worked best involves using a case study–based, action-packed, two- to four-hour class. The class requires executives to work through a case that addresses the key UCD learning points in a progressive-disclosure approach. Table groups compete to come up with the best answers, which they present back to the class. As a result, they "discover" UCD with an absolute minimum of traditional "teaching."

Introductory

After people have seen some of the awareness-type material discussed previously, they're often interested in learning more. In fact, all members of a product group that will be using UCD need more education and training than the basic awareness material. They need introductory education in UCD. This typically takes the form of a one-day class or a Web-based tutorial. Providing this introductory education goes beyond awareness to give examples of how to carry out the various aspects of UCD. The objective here is to make sure that all members of the organization understand and support UCD. For example, the person in the finance department responsible for approving the cost of bringing in users for a UCD activity must know about UCD so that she won't disapprove of the expense in favor of what she may consider a "more worthy" expenditure. Introductory education is also what all UCD multidisciplinary teams need to take before they start on a UCD project.

Advanced

Following the introductory education in UCD, team members also need to take advanced education. This typically takes the form of a two-day workshop in which the various members of the multidisciplinary design team learn about their individual roles, what they can expect from each other, and their responsibilities as a team. This team education is very important because it often is the first time team members are working with members from other disciplines. Team members are often surprised at the perception they have of each other's disciplines. Workshop exercises reinforce the key learning points via experiential learning.

Other types of advanced education may include specific classes on particular methods or techniques. For example, the entire team may want to take a task analysis class if that is an area requiring additional attention. Or a class on user interface design techniques may be of particular interest.

Larger organizations may want to develop their own classes so that they can customize them to their specific needs. However, other organizations may want to bring in education such as this from specialists. A number of vendors provide UCD education. The specific courses discussed here for our Integrated UCD approach are available from IBM (see the Services section of the IBM ease of use website at *www.ibm.com/easy*).

Get On "Every Train Leaving the Station" _____

If you consider all opportunities to advance UCD in your company as trains leaving a station, you should be planning to board every one of those trains to significantly increase your chances of success. Guard against the temptation to evaluate options and choose only one route. If that one route doesn't pan out, then your whole introduction of UCD will fail. You may think that you can get on the next train if one route doesn't pan out; however, this serial approach to introducing UCD simply takes too long. Most companies are already significantly behind where their customers would like to see them in terms of ease of use. The fastest route to getting greater ease of use is, therefore, the most desirable.

If your company is doing process reengineering, get your UCD-related material into the discussions and into the process documentation. In this way, if the process reengineering campaign succeeds, your UCD efforts will, too. You should pursue anything that can further integrate UCD into the very fabric of your organization.

On the other hand, many process reengineering efforts have been spectacular failures. Don't tie UCD to a sinking project. It will sink with it. Be sure to understand that UCD and enterprise engineering are related but different efforts. Building awareness of the user into the product and building awareness of the enterprise as product are related. The best case could be a UCD effort that precedes an enterprise engineering effort in that it creates a mindset and builds a set of skills that carry over into the enterprise design.

An example of how UCD can be integrated into a product development process is illustrated in Figure 3.7. The most important elements to integrate are the key activities that need to occur at specific periods throughout the development process and critical information from UCD activities that need to be used for decision making at certain times. In this example, decision checkpoints (DCPs) are basic business review meetings at which funding allocations are determined and project progress is checked. Any midcourse corrections are determined at these points. These DCPs are ideal for reviewing key UCD activity plans and core UCD metrics. For example, if a task analysis hasn't been carried out, senior management will be aware of this at the Concept DCP and can ensure that it is carried out prior to the project getting the remaining funds to develop the product.

Other areas you should consider include approaches to standardizing performance plans and executive compensation, efforts to improve awards, and endeavors to refocus corporate and product positioning.

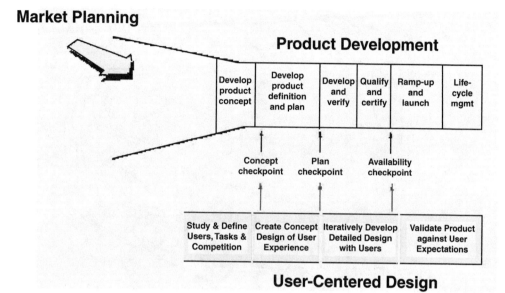

FIGURE 3.7
Integrating UCD into the product development process. (Courtesy of IBM.)

Incorporating UCD metrics into performance plans and executive compensation plans can be powerful influencers as are awards to recognize significant ease of use achievements. Building ease of use and UCD into corporate and product positioning and, in turn, advertising campaigns can be an excellent vehicle from which to introduce and deploy UCD.

In short, the key here is to ensure that you consider any or all efforts that may already be going on within your organization as a means by which to introduce and deploy UCD with a minimum of effort.

CASE STUDY: A UCD TRAINING CLASS

- To be successful, UCD requires cooperation from all key disciplines.
- "Turf" issues may prevent cooperation with a UCD effort.
- UCD champions can help address lack of cooperation.

In one UCD training class, we asked the project teams to draw a cartoon depicting their fears about ways the UCD effort could fail. One team drew the cartoon in Figure 3.8. The character on the train is exclaiming, "Nobody Told Development!" The team explained that the development organization (programmers, technical architects) had the most to lose from UCD with regard to their control over the

FIGURE 3.8
Illustration of the UCD train drawn by students in a UCD class.

product, and so might not support UCD. In fact, very few developers attended the UCD training class, thereby reinforcing this team's fear.

To implement UCD successfully on a wide scale, all key players must be involved. They must be aware of the presence of any "turf" issues. Enlisting the aid of a UCD champion from the various divisions to address these issues is an excellent way to ensure full cooperation in the UCD process (see a discussion of UCD champions later in this chapter). A champion can be a role model first by seeking UCD education and then by advocating a UCD approach. A champion can also give UCD "teeth" by requiring UCD training and implementation.

CASE STUDY: INTEGRATING UCD INTO EXISTING PROCESSES

- Traditional technology-centered development processes can be enhanced by including UCD.

- UCD concepts should not simply be added to existing processes; instead, they should be carefully integrated.
- A robust development process that includes UCD can meet the needs of the entire UCD team.

IBM previously used a technology-centered approach to product development. Development process descriptions made only a passing reference to UCD issues. However, in the mid-1990s, IBM became aware of the importance of UCD. It redefined product development processes to include UCD. The process for IBM Global Services consultants was updated as well. This effort involved integrating UCD into the existing process in a logical, meaningful way. For example, where the traditional process referred to use cases (a largely system-centered concept), the concept and techniques of task analysis were included. However, they were not simply added, but rather integrated with the concept of use cases. Therefore, instead of programmers following one process and designers following another, a UCD team follows a single process that meets the needs of team members of all disciplines.

Get the Right and Best Skills

Effective multidisciplinary design can only happen if the right and best skills for the project are identified and recruited onto the project. All other aspects of the organization may be appropriately primed for UCD, but, without the right people, the project may still fail.

When organizations first find out about UCD, they frequently want to assemble the infrastructure to enable UCD. This desire often translates into measuring the physical dimensions of a UCD laboratory to build one within their organization. However, the physical UCD laboratory is among the least important ingredients in the recipe for UCD success. Ultimately, the most critical ingredients are getting the right people and the best skills. The roles and requisite skills for members of a UCD multidisciplinary design team were outlined in Chapter 2. Each role must be identified and recruited onto the team; each individual must have the best possible skills.

Common problems experienced when establishing a UCD team include the following:

- Traditional organizations often fail to see the value of including visual designers, believing instead that they really only need human factors specialists.

- "New media" companies often fail to see the value of including human factors specialists and believe that they really only need visual designers.

- Many teams fail to realize that marketing must be a core member of the multidisciplinary design team. They assume that marketing can get involved after the product is built.

- Many organizations fail to recruit appropriate individuals to serve as UCD project leaders or user experience design leads. They either assign individuals who lack the requisite skills, or they fail to assign anyone at all, assuming that someone else on the team can take on this responsibility in addition to his other role.

- Organizations not familiar with skills such as visual design or human factors either expect that other specialists will be able to pick up these skills or hire individuals with these skills but with insufficient training and experience. These skills are in high demand within the industry. Organizations shouldn't underestimate what may be required to attract and retain the most desirable candidates.

Ineffective use of UCD is often caused by one of these problems or another related one. These problems can be avoided if appropriate attention is given to filling the roles on the team with individuals who have the best possible skills in each of the discipline areas. An excellent way to avoid these problems is to hire a consulting organization to help you get started and, especially, to provide the requisite experienced specialized skills. After the first successful project or two, work can start on acquiring and building these skills within the organization. Consultants can often help with this as well.

After the appropriate skills have been recruited, it is important to understand effective team structure for UCD as shown in Figure 3.9. With UCD, there is essentially a split between design and production. The key design specialists on the UCD team work closely with specific production counterparts. For example, there is a linkage between a technology architect and a corresponding team of developers or engineers. Other specialists, such as the visual designer, work with production counterparts, such as graphics and animation production specialists. Very small teams may not have a design/production distinction, but most large projects should have these distinct specialists. There is a tendency to blur design and production when the same individuals do both. This tendency often results in a situation where design happens (if it happens at all) just short of implementation and brings with it major problems, including the lack of a coherent and consis-

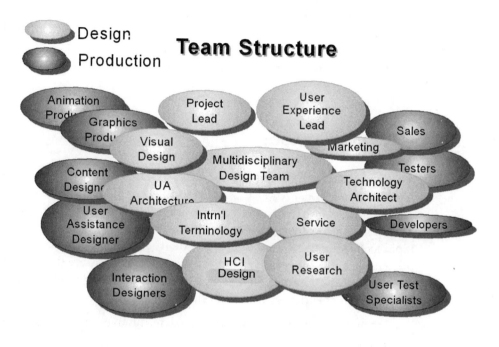

FIGURE 3.9
Team structure. (Courtesy of IBM.)

tent overall design. It is important to consider design not only as a distinct phase and activity but also as a skill distinct from production.

CASE STUDY: SKILL NEEDS

- Reviewing the composition of the multidisciplinary team prior to embarking on a project is essential.
- Examine the team for role presence, confusion, or duplication.
- Identify action items specifically aimed at assembling all the right and best skills.

During UCD kickoff education, one of the activities we engage in with the multidisciplinary design teams is a "have/need" analysis. Immediately after discussing the UCD process, we discuss adapting UCD to meet the needs of the specific product under development. We refer to a template that lists and defines all the UCD roles (e.g., marketing, visual design, HCI design). We discuss each role in relation to the actual product the team will be designing. We identify who on the team will be fulfilling each role. We then determine whether any key skills are missing from the current team configuration. We also discuss role duplication. On several occasions, we have uncovered role duplication (and even triplication!), role confusion (team members unsure of what their roles were), and, most frequently, the absence of key roles. These discussions led to action items aimed at reconfiguring the multidisciplinary team so that all the right skills were present from the very beginning of the project.

Include the Right Methods

Another area where many mistakes occur in introducing UCD involves the selection of methods. With UCD, one size does not fit all. Make sure that you select a core set of UCD methods that will provide information on user tasks and environment, their current ways of carrying out their tasks, iterative rapid feedback on low- and then high-fidelity prototypes, focused and comprehensive hands-on testing, and post-ship feedback. Ensure that guidelines are in place to determine when particular activities are appropriate given the type of product and stage of the development cycle.

Common problems experienced when determining particular UCD methods include the following.

- Assuming that UCD is the same as usability engineering and that all it really comes down to is doing usability testing. This mistaken assumption results in "design by testing," an approach that is not only very expensive because it leads to excessive rework but also is very ineffective. It doesn't address understanding users or evaluating total solution design.

- Deciding that understanding users' methods for completing their tasks is all that is necessary to design a product. Market research organizations often argue for this type of approach. However, this decision leads to a failure to include design feedback of any sort, even though it provides good information with which to design a product.

- Adopting "discount" methods of evaluation that involve professional staff reviewing the product from the user's perspective. This approach excludes the user and should not be used in place of proper user-based methods. These methods can be used as an adjunct to other UCD methods.

- Deciding to do only one UCD activity for a product cycle due to cost. For example, you may decide to collect customer requirements but not to form a UCD team or conduct usability testing. This approach inevitably leads to failure and can provide UCD skeptics with an excuse for never trying UCD again. As pointed out in Chapter 5, there are a variety of alternative ways of carrying out any of the methods of UCD, some of which are very quick and inexpensive. There is no excuse for not collecting the right information on a project.

- Basing decisions on a "pet" customer—one customer who is sometimes, but not always, in close proximity to the vendor or who has some other special relationship wherein that customer's perceptions drive the design. This approach is particularly dangerous where systems require customization for local agency needs. Concentrating on usability with the voice of the pet in the ear often results in a "provincial" product. Customer scope is critical.

The essential message here is that all three of the core types of UCD methods—understanding users, evaluating design, and performing hands-on testing of competitiveness—need to be included in every project.

Case Study: Fitting UCD Activities to a Current Project

- UCD is not "one size fits all" with regard to which methods to implement.
- Investigation can reveal the existence of data that a team may not have known was available.
- Organizational links can help secure access to data from external sources.

One of the most important activities that occurs during a project kickoff is planning the UCD activities necessary for the successful implementation of UCD for that project. When mentoring new UCD teams, it is important to point out that UCD is not a one-size-fits-all process, and that UCD must be customized to meet the needs of any individual project. To facilitate this planning, we use a Sample UCD Plan table. This table contains a list of all possible UCD activities, inputs to these activities, and expected deliverables. During a kickoff, each of these activities is discussed in relation to the current project. For example, during the kickoff for a database product development effort, the team discovered that, contrary to what they had initially believed, they did have access to market data and user requirements applicable to their current target market. An external organization responsible for product marketing had already gathered a wealth of data pertinent to the target market. In this case, the team decided they did not need to gather market data, but, rather, that they did need to put into place an interface between the UCD team and the external marketing organization. Similarly, the team discovered that user requirements had already been collected through multiple efforts by multiple organizations. In this case, the team decided to gather all these disparate requirements into a single location.

They planned to "scrub" (eliminate duplicates, clarify the language, eliminate those that were not within the scope of the project) these user requirements and have users rank them and add new or missing requirements.

Carefully Select a Pilot Project

Some organizations get so interested in getting started after having gone through UCD education that they want to start deploying UCD on all projects at the same time. This approach is usually a mistake. Other organizations may be uncertain about the value of UCD and want proof that it works before they invest in it.

Experience suggests that first running a pilot project will yield the best results. The pilot project should be carefully selected on the basis of having opportunity to make a significant impact on the design, having the key skills available on the team, and being reasonably small and self-contained. A successful pilot project is often one of the best ways to deploy UCD further in an organization. On the other hand, hasty deployment on a less than desirable project can destroy all chances of appropriately introducing UCD to an organization in the future.

Common problems organizations experience in selecting an appropriate pilot project follow.

- Going with the first project suggested by someone in the organization without scrutinizing its appropriateness as a pilot.
- Selecting a project that is "high risk" either because it is a new technology or because it is already late or over budget.
- Working with a project that has multiple dependencies such as third-party suppliers or multiple development sites.

Subsequent projects can accommodate any of these factors, but they should not be a part of the first project in which UCD is used within the company. The project should be representative of the company's typical projects, but it should have characteristics that will ensure its success within a short period.

After the pilot is started, it is also a good idea to provide updates to the company staff with regard to the progress of the project, including key learning experiences that the team thinks are significant. When the project is complete and a success, details of the project, including the indicators of its success, should be shared widely across the company. This communication should include having the members of the design team communicating their own perspectives of UCD and the product success.

CASE STUDY: PILOT PROJECT

- A highly visible, successful pilot project can have a great positive effect on a company's reputation for being user centered.
- Iterative prototyping affords many opportunities to improve a design prior to implementation.
- The total customer experience of an offering includes the user interface, user assistance, such as reference cards, and even human assistance.

By 1997, UCD was being practiced at all of IBM's development labs. Global Services, which includes the huge consulting arm of the corporation, was the next division at IBM poised to begin implementing UCD. The project chosen for the pilot had extremely high visibility—the intranet system for the 1998 Nagano Olympic Games.

In the spring of 1997, a multidisciplinary team was assembled across timezones and cultures consisting of UCD professionals from experienced development labs in San Jose, California; Tucson, Arizona; Warwick, England; and Yamato, Japan. Their goal was to create a walk-up-and-use product for a target audience of 80,000 users, including the press, athletes, and coaches. The product was to support three languages (English, Japanese, and French). They started with two existing prototypes and did work to choose the best choice and enhance that choice through a combination of UCD user studies. Improvements were made at every turn. Changes included making the text and graphics larger, standardizing and simplifying cues to hyperlinks, and modifying graphics and text for drop-down lists and search functions. After it was running, the UCD team then helped to train 200 volunteers who were to help users access the 1300 workstations. They also produced a quick-reference guide—a pocket-sized manual in the three official languages. The team even assisted users at the games themselves.

The success of this project was measured both in client and end user satisfaction. The head of technology for the International Olympic Committee thanked IBM for its role in making the Winter Games "the Games of high technology, with the human touch." Further, user surveys indicated an extremely high satisfaction rating.

Identify a Champion _____

Given that UCD typically isn't a natural fit for a company in the information technology industry, the introduction of UCD into an organization requires care and nurturing. One of the most effective ways to keep the focus is to identify UCD or ease of use champions. The following are desirable characteristics that should be used in selecting individuals to be champions:

- Holds a position in the company
- Is influential
- Is a leader
- Is a change agent

The following is a sample job description for a UCD champion: "The UCD champion is responsible for leading the company/division's drive to UCD and ease of use and for working closely with the corporate leaders to coordinate and optimize companywide UCD deployment and execution."

Advocate for Ease of Use and UCD

The UCD champion is responsible for making the executives, division general managers, and functional areas aware of UCD and for providing them with the appropriate education. The leader drives UCD into the business and is responsible for ensuring the quality and execution of action plans.

The division UCD champion should be an experienced senior individual and will be a member of the investment board to review funding, staffing, resources, salaries, awards, job levels, and attrition.

Performance Plans

The UCD champion is responsible for working with corporate executives to ensure that performance plan commitments (for executives and managers) contain appropriate UCD actions and ease of use targets. It is critical that all groups in an organization be held accountable for UCD, and not just those traditionally responsible for usability. UCD must be pervasive and integrated to be effective. The objectives also include ensuring that UCD practitioners' skills are continually strengthened through internal and external contacts (e.g., education, conferences, workshops, and newsletters).

Specialist Knowledge

The UCD champion should have knowledge of UCD, including the multiple disciplines required to design ease of use into the total customer experience as well as the user feedback methods, tests, and metrics to gather, analyze, and interpret user information. The UCD champion should also be aware of the basis of human factors, stay up to date with industry trends, and participate in companywide activities. The champion must know where to find additional resources from other parts of the company and from third parties and share this knowledge freely with the companywide team of practitioners.

Tracking

The UCD champion is responsible for tracking key UCD metrics, providing reports to executives, bringing key messages and areas for attention to line management, and tracking actions to conclusion.

So, you must choose an executive or senior-level professional who is particularly supportive of the UCD effort and provide this person with the material to help manage UCD in the company from the top. Include presentation material on UCD, together with supporting presentation notes. Also consider providing a project summary template that teams can use to report on project progress, including user feedback information.

The advocates of UCD within the organization should be intimately involved in the pilot project to increase the likelihood of success.

Optimize Your Organization Structure _____

Although you can get started with UCD without addressing organizational structure, the success of the effort can be dramatically enhanced with such a focus. Unless your organization is very small or has only one or two products, organizational structure considerations are important. Companies that have used UCD for some time tend to gravitate to one of two organizational models—centralized or noncentralized. The centralized model has all the professionals of a particular specialization (e.g., visual designers) in one central group. Individuals within the group are assigned to particular projects. One advantage of this model is that it keeps the specialized groups of professionals together and allows them to be flexible with regard to assignment to projects. However, there are disadvantages. The specialists are not really considered equals by the product organization and thereby are not perceived to be part of the core team. In the noncentralized model, professionals from all the specialization areas report directly into product organizations. This model addresses the disadvantages of the centralized model but introduces a new disadvantage. Specialists in this model have little contact with their discipline peers for the purposes of technical vitality and career development. Product managers typically lack an understanding of the unique needs of their specialists, which often leads to employee dissatisfaction.

A third model addresses the disadvantages of both the centralized and noncentralized models while retaining the advantages of both models. The UCD matrix model, as shown in Figure 3.10, involves having all disciplines assigned to particular projects while remaining part of specific discipline Centers of Competence. The Centers of Competence provide employees with technical vitality and career development. These centers also are a source of information regarding which specialists may be the most appropriate for upcoming projects. In large companies, a database of these details on the individual specialists can aid in the selection of professionals for projects. Four Centers of Competence have been identified as being in particular need of this type of structure: visual and industrial design, human-computer interaction, user assistance, and user research. These disciplines are the most responsible for usability of the product, are typically the weakest with regard to political clout, and learn the greatest proportion of their skills through interaction with peers in their discipline. Other disciplines such as marketing and development typically have sufficient organizational support and are usually the central disciplines of the company. A recent study by Mao et al. (2001) substantiates the effectiveness of this approach.

Ensure That Your Specialized Staff Stay Technically Vital

Consider a typical scenario. An organization that is getting started with UCD hires one or more specialists to augment the skills that exist in the organization. These experts, however, quickly become dissatisfied and inefficient. What's missing? A focus on maintaining the technical vitality of these types of specialists is critical to long-term success in carrying out UCD.

The marketplace for these skills is very competitive, and a dissatisfied employee can relatively quickly find a new job elsewhere. User research/ human factors specialists and visual designers, for example, need to keep up technically (e.g., attending conferences and workshops and participating in online discussion groups). They also need to be given work assignments and responsibilities that are challenging and interesting. If particular projects lack these ingredients, you may consider assigning additional work specifically to provide this opportunity. For example, at one company that had relatively uninteresting products from a visual design point of view, the manager assigned the visual designer the role of creating a product Web

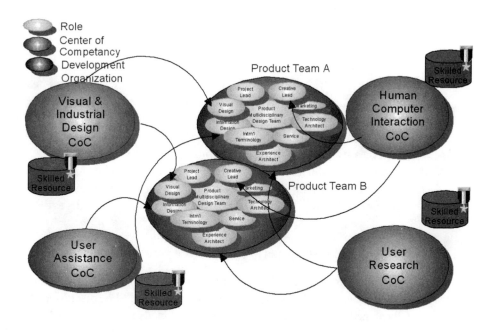

FIGURE 3.10
UCD matrix model. (Courtesy of IBM.)

page and allowed her relative freedom in its design. This resulted in a satisfied, valued employee staying with the company. In addition, the company got a great new product Web site!

Secure Appropriate Funding

Key to the successful introduction of UCD is securing appropriate funds to get started. One of the most common mistakes is to assume that UCD can be done with no dedicated funding. Although this is not true, additional funding may not be necessary. Rather, a reallocation of funds from another part of the organization may provide the needed resources. At one company, a part of the market research budget was reallocated to the "getting started with UCD" budget. The development team was delighted with the results.

The funding that is required typically involves staffing, tools, infrastructure, competitive product acquisition, participant expenses, and project plan support. Each of these areas will be discussed in turn.

Staffing

Staffing typically involves augmenting existing development teams with skills such as visual design and user research/human factors. Experience suggests that an organization should have one person with each of these skills per major project. Some smaller projects may be handled on a part-time basis by one of these professionals; however, larger projects may have five to ten specialists in each of these areas on the team. As pointed out earlier, individuals with these skills are in high demand, so make sure that you have flexibility in your budget to attract the most qualified people.

Tools and Infrastructure

To realize the benefits of an optimized version of UCD as discussed in this book, tools will be required. These tools will be discussed further in Chapter 5. Some amount of infrastructure is also required, including a UCD laboratory. Although some companies use elaborate labs, a simple setup is often quite sufficient. The next section will provide information on a typical lab setup.

Competitive Product Acquisition

Competitive evaluation is a core aspect of our approach to UCD. As such, a critical financial requirement is acquiring the key competitive products for user testing. In some cases, this is a trivial part of the budget if the type of products your organization develops are mass-market, relatively inexpensive ones. However, if the products are high-end, extremely expensive products, you must either plan to have sufficient funds available to purchase the product or use some creative alternatives. You may want to determine whether other parts of your company have already purchased a copy of the product. Most large companies are both developers and purchasers of products like these. A copy of the product you're interested in may already be in the organization somewhere. Another possible option involves using a third-party vendor that may have a copy of the product and could, for a fee, conduct or make the product available so that you can conduct the competitive evaluation.

When doing any competitive evaluation, you must carefully read the license agreement for the product to make sure that your use of the product for evaluation is in keeping with the text of the agreement. It is also a good practice to have your company lawyers look at the license.

If none of these alternative options for acquiring an expensive competitive product is possible, you must ensure that you have sufficient funds to purchase the product yourself. Even if purchasing this product involves a significant amount of money, the benefits gained will no doubt justify the expenditure. In one case, an executive, when dealing with an organization that was facing this problem, argued that if a development team didn't think that spending the money to intimately understand the competitive product was worthwhile, then it probably shouldn't be trusted with the development funds assigned to them. After pointing this out to the team, the product organization promptly purchased the competitor's product, conducted a thorough UCD competitive evaluation, and, as a result, developed a far superior product.

Participant Expenses

UCD tends to rely on a regular supply of user feedback study participants. As a result, a budget allocation for funds to provide reimbursement for these participants must be contemplated. Four types of expenses are typically involved in UCD studies regarding participants: recruiting, reimbursing Web participants, reimbursing lab participants, and providing other expenses incurred regarding lab participants.

Recruiting.   Participants can be recruited using a search firm or a Web site database and dedicated staff person. A search firm can use either customer lists provided by you or a variety of purchased lists as a starting point for a search for your designated target audience. The latter is preferred when you also want to include users currently using your competitor's product in the studies. Such firms identify the potential candidates, call them to determine who is interested, and then schedule them to suit your test schedule. If you're using a Web site database and your own staff, you need to advertise and encourage potential participants to sign up with your recruiting database by giving them an incentive. The incentive can be a random drawing for a popular product, developed by your company or another company. For example, IBM has run a "Win a ThinkPad" contest as the incentive for its recruiting database. Lotus runs a monthly drawing for a copy of its office productivity product set, SmartSuite. Other giveaways have included products like digital cameras and hand-held computers.

Instead of products, it is also possible to simply use money, that is, pay every person who puts his or her name in your recruiting database a set amount of money for doing so. A particularly creative and successful approach used recently involves providing participants with the option of contributing to a charity of their choice in exchange for their participation.

In addition to using the Web site database as a source of potential participants, you can also use the product registration information available in your company. After you have a list, when you're not using a search firm, you still need to have a member of your staff contact the candidates, determine their interest, and then schedule those who are interested in participating in your studies. This search is typically done by contract staff but can also sometimes be done using a portion of the time of your regular staff. The work is rather tedious and, as a result, not particularly well suited to highly trained UCD specialists.

Web Participants. In addition to recruiting expenses, participants also need to be reimbursed or at least thanked for participating. In the early days of Web-based surveys, it was possible to run relatively short surveys with no reimbursement. A thank you e-mail note was all that was expected. Now, however, with many more of these activities happening on the Web, high response rates to surveys require some amount of reimbursement. The type of thank-you reimbursement you choose will depend on the length of the survey, how difficult it is to get respondents to complete it, and what proportion of the total number of people you know about that you would like to have respond. A short survey to a fairly wide audience with a relatively low response rate needed could use a thank-you gift of something like a mouse pad or tote bag. A larger survey to a more specialized audience where a higher response rate is needed may require a thank-you gift such as $50 to $100 per respondent or a random drawing involving a much more expensive item, such as an all-expense-paid vacation or a more expensive product. As mentioned previously, other ideas include giving respondents the option of designating particular charities as the recipients of their reimbursement for participating. Whatever type of reimbursement you decide to adopt for a particular study or series of studies, keep in mind what is involved in getting it to participants. Gifts such as mouse pads are easier to send than bulky items such as t-shirts and coffee mugs.

During these studies you must maintain a "fatigue database" of respondents. Because administering surveys is quite easy, many customers are constantly bombarded with requests. If too many of these requests come from a single source, customers can become dissatisfied, annoyed, or even angry at the constant intrusion. Therefore, companies should keep a centralized database of participants indicating which surveys they have taken part in. Coordination among divisions (e.g., hardware, software, and services) should ensure that only one survey is sent when a customer makes a purchase. Finally, a good rule of thumb is to not survey any single respondent more often than once every six months.

One last consideration that must be dealt with when selecting a method of thanking respondents is whether each participant will get something or whether all participants get a chance to win something bigger. If you choose the latter, you must consult the sweepstakes and lottery laws. Each state within the United States has its own laws pertaining to contests like these, and countries around the world also have their own individual laws. Contact your company lawyer for further information about these laws.

Lab Participants.   The expenses incurred with participants who visit your UCD lab in person can be much higher than for surveys and other remote techniques. In this case, you may have to plan for the expense of travel and accommodations for participants who are from out of town, meals and breaks during the session, and reimbursement for participating. The amount of the travel expense will depend on how close your facility is to a representative population of customers. The reimbursement can be similar to what was discussed in the previous section. The difference with participants attending in person is that these sessions are typically longer, and it takes the participant more effort to attend. The amount of the reimbursement or the value of the thank-you gift should reflect this. Reimbursements and gifts will also differ for the type of participant selected for your activities. For example, you need to give a database administrator much more than you give a data entry clerk. Also, if you're finding it difficult to recruit participants, you may want to increase the rate of reimbursement.

Project Plan Support

A common mistake made by organizations just getting started with UCD involves establishing adequate funding but failing to plan for the impact of the greater focus on UCD and ease of use on the project plan itself. There are two important factors to consider here. The first factor involves determining up front what the major ease of use objectives will be for the new product or release and then using these objectives to get a design and development sizing of the effort to implement these objectives in the product. This sizing should be reflected in the product plan. The second factor to consider involves planning for the resource that will be required throughout the development cycle to make changes based on user feedback. No modern product can be designed completely at the start of the project and then be developed based on this frozen design. Instead, with UCD, a very good concept design is created with customer input at the start of the project. The concept design is subsequently iterated throughout the remainder of the development cycle. Given good up-front work, less rework is required later in the cycle, so changes tend to be less resource intensive. However, changes must be made throughout the cycle, and the resource required to make them must be made available and planned for.

You should determine your market objectives for the product and then set your user problem fix rate (the percentage of known problems you will fix) accordingly. (See Table 3.1.) Using the definition of user problem severity provided in Table 3.2, you could use the following fix rates for the various ease of use market objectives.

TABLE 3.1
User problem fix rate by market objective

Market Objective	Level 1	Level 2	Level 3
Be market leader	100%	100%	90%
Meet competition	100%	90%	65%
Maintain status	100%	80%	50%

The definition of the three severity levels follows.

TABLE 3.2
User problem severity level

Severity	Description
Level 1	Users are unable to continue with a task, or series of tasks, due to the problem
Level 2	Users have considerable difficulty completing a task, or series of tasks, but are eventually able to continue
Level 3	Users have minor difficulty completing a task, or series of tasks

For instance, a project that elects to adopt a "be-market-leader" level must plan to fix all Level 1 and 2 user problems identified in UCD studies, and 90% of the Level 3 problems. A project targeting a maintain-status level would have to plan to fix all Level 1 problems but only 80% of the Level 2 and 50% of the Level 3 problems.

Ensuring that your plans anticipate fixing problems at these rates will guarantee that problems will be fixed even if they surface later in the development cycle. Without this type of planning, a very small proportion of the problems identified later in the development cycle are likely to be fixed.

Create the Infrastructure

We pointed out earlier that some organizations just starting with UCD tend to focus too quickly on building a UCD laboratory and don't focus on other important factors, such as getting the right and best skills and securing appropriate funding. However, when some progress has been made on these latter factors, it is also advisable to focus on building the requisite infrastructure.

UCD Lab

Test Participant Rooms   A typical UCD lab setup includes separate rooms for the test participants and the observers (Figure 3.11). The participant rooms are typically configured to simulate the environment in which the product would most likely be used. This may be an office, a cubicle, a bank teller station, a bank of airplane seats, an automobile, or a family living room. The closer the test environment is to the actual one, the more accurate the tests will be. There can be one or more participant rooms, depending on how many sessions typically need to be run simultaneously. The participant rooms also have cameras used to capture the participants' facial expressions, their hand movements, their use of manuals, and the activity on their computer screens. The latter camera is often replaced by a scan converter, which captures information from the screen directly and stores it on videotape. A new tool, which will be described in Chapter 5, actually eliminates the need for a camera for capturing screen activity by recording the session in software. When cameras are used, they are sometimes hidden from view, mounted in the ceiling.

Observation Rooms   A one-way glass typically separates the observation room from the participant room. (See Figure 3.12.) The glass allows observers to study what the participants are working on in the adjacent room. If the lights are dimmed in the observation room, the participants cannot see into the observation room. Additionally, the rooms are sound-resistant so that observers won't disturb the participants while they work. When

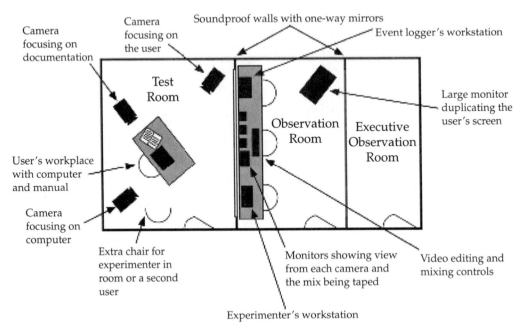

FIGURE 3.11
Floor plan of a typical UCD laboratory. (Adapted from Nielsen, 1993.)

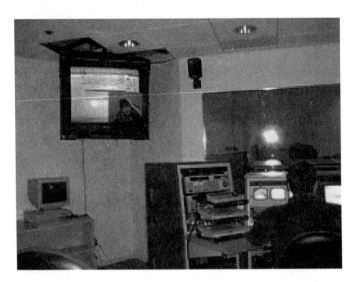

FIGURE 3.12
An observation room looking onto a test participant room. (Courtesy of IBM.)

FIGURE 3.13
A usability lab room for groups. (Courtesy of IBM.)

the observer needs to ask participants a question or to direct them to move onto another task, a microphone on the control panel or on a headset worn by the observer is used.

To ensure that all the observers are able to see what is going on in the participant room, there is often a large monitor or two in the observation room. The monitor usually shows two inputs, the participant's computer screen and his or her face. Audio speakers are strategically placed so observers can hear what the participant is saying.

In many usability labs, there is also a room for gathering feedback from groups of users (Figure 3.13). These rooms are used for efficiently collecting feedback from 10 to 20 users simultaneously as well as for testing products intended to be used by groups of users.

Control Panel   A core element of the UCD lab is the control panel located in the observation room. (See Figure 3.14.) It typically includes a scan converter to capture the participant's computer screen image. Make sure to purchase a scan converter that is capable of capturing the screen resolutions you will be using. The scan converter allows you to zoom in on parts of the participant's computer screen. As pointed out earlier, a new tool, which will be described in Chapter 5, actually eliminates the need for a scan converter by capturing the screen activity directly by computer. The cameras used to capture the participants' experiences in the test participant rooms

FIGURE 3.14
A control panel. (Courtesy of IBM.)

are recorded on VCR decks that form part of the control panel. The control panel also typically includes a video editing suite that is sometimes used to create summary videotapes of studies used to present to management and development teams. Although teams in a highly mature UCD organization use summary tapes less frequently, they are invaluable in the early stages. The mixing board allows practitioners to merge two or more tapes with the computer screen and participant videos. Additionally, the mixing board comes with a time-code generator connected to the mixer that stamps the time on the tape. The time stamps ensure that the logging of the sessions by practitioners and the various videotapes stay in sync.

An alternative, or occasionally an adjunct, to a fixed UCD lab is a portable lab. Several vendors provide prebuilt or custom-developed portable labs that can be taken on the road with relative ease to allow testing at workplaces or conferences. Some of these labs are wireless for flexibility and convenient setup.

Track Progress _____

Don't take your eye off of the ball after things get going with UCD deployment. It is all too easy for an organization to be enthusiastic at the start, plan to do everything right, and then hit the reality of cost constraints, time-to-market pressures, and other factors. To keep the focus, it is important to hold regular reviews of deployment progress, as well as detailed reviews of progress on particular projects. A variety of core metrics that can be used to track progress were outlined in Chapter 2.

Recognize and Celebrate Success

Organizations often fail to recognize and celebrate success appropriately. Some people in any organization are bound to be skeptical of any new approach. Consequently, when projects using UCD yield real business success, this fact should be widely communicated and celebrated. Each positive trade press report citing ease of use enhancements should be sent around the company, posted on bulletin boards, and framed in executive offices. The team responsible for the success should be given appropriate awards and other recognition. When others in the organization see this success, they will also want to do everything in their power to use UCD effectively on their projects.

Communicate, Communicate, Communicate

A final critical success factor when introducing and deploying UCD concerns the quantity and quality of communication. Don't assume that you can get something like UCD started, and then just let it run on its own. Ultimate success depends on continuous communication among professionals on the multidisciplinary design team, between the team and the rest of the development organization, and between the team and executive management.

After your UCD implementation results in successful products, you should also communicate this success to your customers. Go ahead, brag a little! Usability is an important sales message. An example of IBM advertising their focus on UCD is shown in Figure 3.15.

CASE STUDY: COMMUNICATING THE IMPORTANCE OF UCD

- Communication in the form of informal education should be conducted at every opportunity.
- Because management support is vital to the success of UCD, managers should be a primary target for this communication.
- Data helps support the UCD message.

FIGURE 3.15
Poster advertising the importance of UCD. (Courtesy of IBM.)

We consulted on an intranet development project for a notoriously conservative company that had been traditionally slow to adopt new technology. The intranet application under development was far more advanced than anything its employees had ever used before. Up to that time, employees had used a "green screen" (mainframe) application to submit database queries, the results of which were printed at a central location and delivered a day later. The new intranet promised to give employees instant and easy access to data. However, the concept of UCD was new to the management, even to the manager responsible for the project. In fact, this manager wasn't convinced of its value. We met with this manager frequently and used these opportunities to explain the importance of UCD. We "sneaked" education into every discussion. One team member carried a notebook, containing lists of heuristics, an example of cost-justification, and a table of the number of users recommended for usability tests. When an issue arose, relevant reference was always handy. These data helped support the UCD message. The result was a greater awareness of the importance of UCD, additional support for efforts to engage users in the process, and, ultimately, a more usable solution.

The History of UCD at IBM

In order to illustrate how UCD can be introduced at a large company, we describe here how UCD was introduced at IBM.

UCD dramatically improved the ease of use of IBM software and hardware. For example, the workstation database product, DB2 Universal Database, used UCD starting with the 5.0 release of its product. The results of IBM's own studies, business results, and trade press reviews all substantiate the improvements made in ease of use. For example, *PC Week* referred to "a vastly easier client setup procedure, integrated replication and a fresh new interface," and *InfoWorld* pointed out that the "Latest DB2 exceeds competition. . . . Administrative functions are well-integrated into the easy-to-use Control Center interface." *Information Week* wrote that "Installation, on both the server and client, is mind-numbingly easy. . . . Universal Database is breathtaking for its enormous leap into ease of use."

In the area of hardware, UCD was first used for IBM notebook computers, starting with the ThinkPad 770 and 600 models. Again, IBM studies, business results, and trade press reviews point to the improvements made in the ease of use of these models. For example, *Gartner Report* wrote, "If winning in the notebook game is the result of attention to details, the 770 has it in spades, especially when it comes to usability." *PC Magazine* claimed that "The ThinkPad's [600] usability suffers no peer." *PC Computing* similarly echoed, "usability is where this machine truly shines." *Business Week* wrote, "IBM wins my vote for a huge display and excellent ergonomics. . . . The keyboard is the best I have ever seen in a laptop." *PC Week* similarly pointed out that "The Trackpoint is the most useful pointing device we've seen to date on a notebook." It is the business case derived from these types of results that further drives the broad implementation of UCD at IBM.

Origins of UCD at IBM

A human factors organization was first established at IBM in the mid-1950s, and various usability and human factors methods have been used over the years. IBM's version of UCD was developed in the early 1990s. The approach continues to evolve. It has incorporated ideas from IBM project teams via the company's UCD Advisory Council, and from industry peers via the Association for Computing Machinery's Special Interest Group on Computer-Human Interaction (CHI), Usability Professionals' Association (UPA), and Human Factors and Ergonomics Society (HFES) conferences, and standards organizations such as International Standards Organization (ISO), American National Standards Institute (ANSI), and the National Institute for Standards and Technology (NIST) Industry Usability Workshop.

Introduction Strategies

Making the transition from traditional human factors and usability approaches to full-scale UCD involved a major cultural transformation for IBM and a paradigm shift for its practitioners. Several steps were taken to ensure that the key elements of this transition were carried out appropriately. These key elements included identifying core principles, carrying out education, and integrating UCD into the company's business and development process.

Transition

Because UCD represented a significant and substantive change from earlier usability and human factors approaches practiced at IBM, particular focus was given to introducing company employees to the new approach. This focus was especially important, given that all members of a development organization were now responsible for the total customer experience of the product in ways in which they were never previously responsible. To address this new responsibility, an overview presentation was created, including video, and delivered it to all employees via an internal television broadcast and individual development site visits. This presentation was augmented by overview and practitioner information that was made available to all employees via IBM's intranet. Multimedia classes were also developed at both the introductory and advanced levels to teach UCD. A case-based executive workshop was also developed for management teams—executives through project leaders—to provide them with the skills and knowledge required to manage UCD projects. Finally, and perhaps most importantly, UCD principles, methods, and metrics were integrated into the company's business and development process.

Experience to date has shown that, even though all the contributions mentioned so far had an appreciable effect on introducing and deploying UCD, the most significant contributions included articulating core principles, having a set of highly efficient methods, and integrating UCD into the company's business and development process. A common excuse for not integrating UCD into company engineering processes is that there are no agreed-to elements that can be measured and thus managed. IBM developed a core set of UCD metrics that summarize the key elements important in the management of UCD on projects at the project, division, and corporate level. A metrics template can be found on the CD that accompanies this book. A template ensures that organizations use the same information for all products. It includes project information like the individual responsible for the design of the total customer experience, the target audience, prime competitor, and user problem fix targets. Included as well are specific ease of use objectives for the release and targeted ease of use customer satisfaction and their status. Enablement information (e.g., schedule and budget) is reported as is the list of total user problems identified and the fix status of each. A running monthly summary of the top five open user problems and their status is also included. Finally, a summary of the number of hours of UCD studies completed is provided in the categories of understanding users, evaluating designs, and using hands-on testing. Various project, division, and corporate summary reports of these data are run on a regular basis. A template of a summary UCD report is shown in Figure 3.16.

Organization

UCD at IBM is carried out at the product team level by UCD teams. The specialized disciplines of visual design, industrial design, HCI design, and user assistance constitute the core members of the team along with marketing, product development, and support specialists. The project teams are located at our development laboratories worldwide including Austin, Texas, Raleigh, North Carolina, Santa Teresa, California, Poughkeepsie, New York,

Project Information

UCD Project Leader	User Audience	Prime Competitor	Fix Rate Model
?	?	?	?

Ease of Use Objectives

Objective	Validation	Status
?	?	?
?	?	?
?	?	?

User Satisfaction

Baseline	Current	Target	Competitor
?	?	?	?

Enablement

Team	Schedule	Resource	Training	Budget
?	?	?	?	?

User Problem Summary

Severity	Number	% Fixed	Target
1	?	?%	?%
2	?	?%	?%
3	?	?%	?%

Top 5 Open User Problems

Priority	Sev.	Problem Description	Date Identified	Fix Date
1	?	?	?	?
2	?	?	?	?
3	?	?	?	?
4	?	?	?	?
5	?	?	?	?

User Involvement (hours)

Understand	Evaluate	Test	Total
?	?	?	?

FIGURE 3.16
Summary UCD report template. (Courtesy of IBM.)

Dallas, Texas, Rochester, New York, Boulder, Colorado, and San Jose, California, in the United States; Warwick and Hursley in the United Kingdom; Boeblingen in Germany; Rome in Italy; Yamato in Japan; and Toronto and Vancouver in Canada. These teams develop these kinds of products and other offerings.

- **Software:** Personal and group productivity, application development, data management, transaction system, network and Internet software products, via the Lotus, Tivoli, WebSphere, and DB2 brands.
- **Computers:** Personal, mobile, workstation, and network computers such as NetVista, ThinkPad, WorkPad, and IntelliStation.
- **Servers:** Hardware server products and accompanying operating system software products including zSeries, pSeries, iSeries, and xSeries.
- **Components:** Hard drives, tape backup, microprocessors, LAN adapters, printers, and mice.
- **Services:** Offerings that help customers with their information technology needs including managing via outsourcing the entire operation, including a full suite of UCD offerings.

- **Research:** Exploration of new technology frontiers from chip materials to new ways for humans to interact with computers. New product ideas are generated and then transformed into offerings by the product divisions.

Teams

In addition to forming parts of UCD teams, the specialized UCD disciplines also typically report to discipline organizations and are managed using a matrix approach. Performance plans for team members typically include a discipline contribution as well as a contribution to the product.

IBM UCD specialists (i.e., HCI designers, visual/industrial designers, user research specialists) across the company now number in the hundreds, and are increasing steadily. IBM has 25 UCD laboratories worldwide with a total of 78 individual test participant rooms.

Three corporate positions and accompanying organizations have also recently been formed to ensure the attainment of IBM's strategic objectives regarding ease of use. These include a Vice President of Ease of Use, responsible for overall strategy; a Director of Ease of Use Integration, responsible for implementing UCD across the management team; and a corporate User-Centered Design Architect and Team Leader, responsible for IBM's UCD methods, processes, tools, and staff.

Frequently Asked Questions _____

Many people have preconceived notions about what UCD is all about. These notions are often myths that need to be dispelled if UCD is to be introduced effectively. Although many of the activities discussed in this book will help to address these misconceptions, it is important to survey some of the most common myths and provide appropriate responses to them. The following are questions we've encountered most frequently and our answers to them.

What is a Simple Description of UCD?

User-Centered Design is an industry-leading approach for designing competitive ease of use into the total customer experience with products. It ensures that products are not just easy to buy, easy to set up, easy to learn, easy to use, and easy to upgrade but also engaging, intuitive, and integrated. It involves having a multidisciplinary team design the product solution starting with the externals—everything the customer sees, hears, and touches—and gathering continuous user input via UCD feedback methods.

What Is the Distinction Between Ease of Use and UCD?

This distinction confuses many people. Ease of use is an attribute of the product that we're trying to achieve, and UCD is the method to achieve it. Note that ease of use is actually only one of the attributes a team targets for a product when using UCD. All the "ease of's" that we discuss in this book (e.g., ease of learning, ease of installing, ease of using) are also targeted, as are the attributes of engagement, intuitiveness, and integration. All these attributes are important. In fact, it isn't sufficient to simply develop products that are easy to use (e.g., that don't cause user errors). It is now also a requirement to design products that delight users by being fun and enjoyable and that just make you feel good. To use an analogy, healthy used to mean that you didn't have any illnesses, but that isn't the case today. Now, healthy means that you eat right, exercise, and are in shape. The same holds true for product design. Products shouldn't simply work; they also should be a delight to use.

Is the Goal to Have Developers Automatically Incorporate UCD into Their Timeline?

Yes. Just like good hygiene, UCD should become a natural thing to do for all members of an organization, whether software, hardware, or services. Just like you wouldn't leave home without brushing your teeth, all disciplines in an organization shouldn't deliver designs without getting user input on them.

Some People Talk About Usability Testing. Is That the Same Thing as UCD?

Equating usability testing with UCD is another common misconception. Usability testing is one method used within UCD; however, UCD is much more than that. In fact, organizations that simply do usability testing aren't very successful at achieving high levels of ease of use. You must have a strong focus on multidisciplinary design, and not just testing. Furthermore, you should use a variety of methods for getting user input including task analysis, competitive evaluation, design walkthroughs, interactive design evaluations and validations, early-ship surveys, and benchmark assessments. Each method is appropriate for different phases of the product development cycle.

Can You Explain How Certain UCD Tools Can Benefit Designers?

The user input methods of UCD offer a significant benefit to designers, whether the methods are carried out in a UCD lab or UCD tools are used. They provide an understanding of the customer, which is critical for initiating design, as well as providing iterative feedback on designs and alternative designs as they evolve. In our experience, designers often face the challenge of getting particular designs accepted by other members of the development team. A lead architect may express the opinion that he would like to see candy-apple red as the primary background color for an image, rather than the black that the designer came up with. Without customer input, this type of discussion is often based on little more than personal opinion. With customer feedback, however, the customer is the decision maker and final arbiter. The appropriate user-based designs are implemented. After all, the customer will be paying for the product, which will ultimately pay the wages of the entire team. Relying on user input, therefore, makes the life of designers less stressful and more successful.

Is UCD Only Appropriate for Products with Pervasive Graphical User Interfaces?

No. UCD is appropriate for any kind of product a customer is going to use. It is being used in companies to design everything from power station control rooms to toasters.

Doesn't UCD Involve a Lot of Heavy Process and Complicated Methods?

No. The documentation provided on UCD is intended as a guide to collecting the information necessary to provide a good design. A range of methods are available, depending on the type of project. Fundamentally, alignment with the core UCD principles is much more important than faithful adherence to a documented process. In fact, carrying out a process like UCD doesn't guarantee great products, but alignment with the UCD principles does.

Who Needs to Know about UCD in an Organization?

Everyone! Many organizations make a serious mistake in expecting that some dedicated group somewhere will learn UCD and then magically produce wonderful products. The only way to ensure success in producing great products is to encourage all members of an organization to "live and breathe" user data, to provide for excellence in the emerging design of the total customer experience with the product.

Does UCD Involve Decreasing Management Control over Projects?

No, quite the contrary. Management needs to demand customer data, review it regularly, manage design of product externals, and see the user-centered aspects of projects as being as important as, or sometimes more important than, the traditional elements.

Do All Product Teams Need to Invest in UCD at the Same High Level?

Absolutely not. Investment in UCD involves a business decision. Competitive advantage objectives must be made explicit at the start of a project, and these objectives need to inform the level of investment in UCD. There are several models of investment based on type of product, product life cycle, and other factors. In fact, many organizations don't think about this decision enough. Many teams assume that they're aiming for best-of-breed market leadership, even though they may be producing their first product in a market in which they have had very little experience. They also often assume that all projects aim at best-of-breed ease of use. However, this decision doesn't lead to a planning effort capable of sizing the effort necessary to achieve this goal. The assumption is often that ease of use will somehow happen for free, even though other technology-based aspects of products are more appropriately planned for. Product design is a series of tradeoffs. Ease of use goals must be realistic and balanced against other requirements.

What Is Presented in UCD Executive Review Meetings?

Executives should be provided with a high-level overview of the UCD status of a project such as the data in Figure 3.16. This information can be maintained and kept continually available using the UCD metrics tool described in Chapter 5.

How Should Fix Rate Models and Ease of Use Objectives Be Determined?

The product executive management team should determine the overall competitive positioning and strategy for the product that, in turn, sets the fix rate model. The objectives should come from either previous UCD work or market research. Chapter 5 will address this in greater detail.

What Are the Top Five User Problems After You Fix All Level 1 Problems?

The top five user problems should always list the most severe problems that haven't yet been fixed. If, during a release, all are fixed except for a few Level 3 problems, these become the top five user problems. It would be great if all products had to ask this question!

Do User Problems Have to Come from Users?

Although heuristic design reviews can be helpful in identifying problems, "user problems" are those problems that come from users. However, practitioners should use some level of professional judgment in applying this rule. If, for example, a number of user problems all fit within one larger comprehensive category of problem and it is better to solve the higher level problem category, then do so.

What If My Organization Has Four Levels of Severity of Problem?

We've chosen to use three levels of severity for our implementation of UCD. The severity levels are defined in user terms and not system terms. Most existing defect severity systems use a system focus. Therefore, it is often necessary to translate defect tracking system items into UCD user problems anyway, regardless of the levels of severity involved.

What If My Project Doesn't Have a True UCD Multidisciplinary Team?

Although it is desirable for all the members of the various disciplines that are key to UCD to work on one team, they do not need to work in one physical location or even meet regularly face-to-face. The only real requirement is that they must have the specialized skills necessary to design the total customer experience to contribute appropriately to the overall design of the product.

What Is the Difference Between UCD and Market Research?

This is a common question. Fundamentally, market research focuses on an understanding of the market and such factors as high-level requirements, buying triggers, and industry trends. UCD, on the other hand, focuses on an understanding of the customers, their tasks, and their input on iterative designs of the product. In other words, market research determines *what* product should be built, whereas UCD determines *how* it should be designed.

Now that we have reviewed the key elements to consider in introducing User-Centered Design to an organization, examined the development of UCD at IBM, and answered frequently asked questions, we will examine the topic of deploying UCD.

Deploying the Approach 4

This chapter discusses how UCD is deployed to design the total customer experience for hardware, software, and service offerings. Deploying the UCD approach involves implementing a set of activities in a sequence that extends from early planning through to delivery and beyond. These activities can be categorized within the following phases:

- Planning,
- Concept,
- Detailed design and development,
- Life-cycle management.

Linear or Iterative?

Describing UCD as a "sequence" of activities seems to imply that UCD is a linear approach. Linear development approaches, such as the Waterfall process (Figure 4.1), have been popular. These approaches define a set of steps

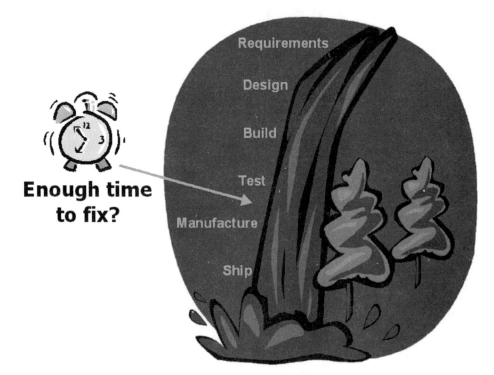

FIGURE 4.1
The waterfall process.

such as requirements gathering, design, implementation, test, and delivery. In linear processes, these steps are discrete and somewhat narrowly defined; consequently, there is a constant forward movement from step to step. For example, when a design is set forth, the assumption is made that the design is complete, so the team moves on to the next phase, which is usually implementation.

A UCD approach can also be considered iterative. Requirements can be refined beyond an initial phase in which they are gathered. Designs evolve by testing them with customers and incorporating the feedback into the design. Even late in the UCD approach, for example, during the beta phase, customer feedback can influence the final deliverable.

However, in fact, UCD is neither linear nor totally iterative. Calling UCD iterative implies to some that the team will never deliver a final product. The image of endless, aimless iteration does not inspire confidence. This description is not accurate by any means. Even though a certain amount of iteration is essential within UCD, there is a definite progression toward a final goal. For example, a UCD team should not embark upon a second requirements gathering phase after the design and development phase. Another example of the sequential nature of UCD is that the team should not be routinely rethinking key high-level design assumptions late in the detailed design phase. In some cases, extreme circumstances, such as a drastic change in the marketplace, have warranted a late-phase design change; however, this practice is not indicative of a typical instance of UCD.

Knowing when to iterate and when to move forward can be facilitated by setting measurable objectives for the design. Objectives should be customer based. If an objective is met, the team can move forward to the next design task.

Now, let's look at the UCD phases and some key activities.

Planning Phase

Before any work can be done to design an offering, a fair amount of planning should be undertaken. It would be extremely risky to begin to design without first ensuring that necessary resources are in place for undertaking the effort, that you know who you're designing the offering for, and that there is, in fact, a potential market for the new offering. The following activities are undertaken during the planning phase:

- Describing market and audience
- Logistical planning
- Requirements gathering and prioritizing
- Sizing and scheduling
- Creating the UCD plan

Describing Market and Audience

Before any work can be done toward designing a new offering, the team must have a clear understanding and definition of the new product from the perspective of the marketplace. Typically, a market planning team provides the initial impetus and direction for the new offering. The team gathers data and defines the new offering from a variety of perspectives, including

- The environment and value sector in which the new offering will be positioned,

- The positioning of the offering with respect to the company's portfolio and overall strategy,
- The target market segments for the offering,
- Some high-level customer requirements for the new offering,
- Competitive offering information,
- New offering objectives.

The UCD team must be closely aligned with the market planning team during this phase of the UCD approach. Data gathered by market planners is shared with the UCD team, which then writes the audience description. Identifying customers and their characteristics makes designers aware of for whom they are designing. This approach sounds obvious, but it is all too often overlooked. In the absence of knowledge about end users, designers often design for people like themselves. This practice is seldom desirable because users typically differ from designers in their skills, task requirements, mental models, and preferences.

The audience often covers a wider spectrum than anticipated; in many cases, there will be more than one user class constituting the audience. A *user class* (also called *audience* or *market segment*) is a subset of the customer population whose members are similar in system usage and relevant personal characteristics. Data should be collected on relevant end user attributes such as general or specific technology experience, experience in an application domain, job, other systems operated by the customer, education, motivation, and tasks performed. Each distinct user group should be defined specifically enough that members of that group would recognize themselves by the description. This description can then be used to recruit representative customers for the various data-gathering activities. Here is an example of an audience description: "You are a personal digital assistant (PDA) user. You have owned and used a PDA for at least 6 months. You use your PDA, on average, about three times a day. You use your PDA for recording and referring to phone numbers, your schedule, and note taking. You transfer data between your PDA and desktop or laptop computer at least weekly."

A given task may be performed by more than one class of user. For example, booking a room in a hotel reservation system may be performed by a desk clerk, a supervisor, or a trainee. Requirements should be developed for each distinct user class.

The user classes include direct users of the system, indirect users, and remote users. *Direct users* are those who actually operate the system. A desk clerk is a direct user of a hotel management system. She or he will have operational requirements for the system. *Indirect users* are those who ask others to operate the system for them and make use of the output. The hotel manager may be an indirect user of the hotel management system. The manager may require that the system provide particular information but not access the information directly. A guest is also an indirect user of the hotel management system. They do not use the system directly, for example, but they do require that statements are correct and complete. *Remote users* are those who depend upon the input or output of the system. A travel agent is a remote user of the system accessing it via a Web site.

Logistical Planning

Recruiting. Because UCD relies on gathering data from representative customers, steps must be taken to ensure that participants will be available for the various data-gathering activities, and that these studies are undertaken in a legal manner.

As soon as the team has an audience description, recruiting activities can begin. Lists of potential study participants can be obtained from a variety of sources, including

- Sales contacts,
- Development team members,
- Attendees at education classes on related products,
- Business directories of companies performing the kind of work for which the target product is designed (e.g., accounting firms for a spreadsheet program),
- Temporary employment agencies or suppliers of contractors,
- Recruitment agencies,
- User groups,
- Previous study participants,
- Local conferences,
- Trade shows.

After you have a list of names, conduct a screening process to ensure that the participants' skills or experiences match those of the profile. Screening can be done by using a questionnaire that can be administered by telephone, with e-mail, or over the Internet.

An extremely important consideration that has emerged most prominently of late is participant fatigue. Because the Internet has made surveying customers so easy, customers are finding themselves "oversolicited." By creating and managing a database of participants, it is possible to ensure that no one participant is overused for any data-gathering activity. It is also important to comply with privacy laws when dealing with e-mail and customer information.

Scheduling.   Scheduling the data-gathering sessions can be done by the team or with the help of an administrative assistant. The scheduler should be aware of holidays and of other competing events. Often the recruiter may wish to "overbook" a session to ensure that an adequate number of participants will attend.

Legal Issues.   Attention should be given to having the appropriate paperwork in place to ensure legal and confidential data gathering. Confidentiality agreements, permission-to-videotape forms, and nondisclosure forms protect both the participants and the company. You should also anticipate special cases, such as having parents sign these agreements for their children who participate in data-gathering activities. In the interest of efficiency, it is a good idea to supply these forms to participants beforehand.

Reimbursement.   The team should decide what form of compensation is to be provided to participants. If customers are asked to give up work time to attend a feedback session, the team should consider compensation commensurate with the participant's rate of pay. On the other hand, in many cases, a token gift such as "logowear" or a gift certificate to a local mall will be adequate. (See Chapter 3 for more information on reimbursement.)

Requirements Gathering and Prioritizing

Requirements gathering is the process of finding out what the target audience requires from a product. A variety of techniques can be used to determine these requirements. Some common techniques include interviews, observation, tests of prior versions of the system, and system analysis.

Requirements gathering is concerned not only with determining needs but also with understanding them. This technique gives the designer the knowledge to set functional requirements for the system and also provides information to perform analysis as decisions come up during the design-and-development process. The result of requirements gathering is a representation of the problems with the current offering and the requirements for the new offering.

There are two categories of product requirements. *Functional requirements* specify what the product must do. *User requirements* specify what the users want the product to do. User requirements often specify the acceptable level of user performance and satisfaction with the system.

Functional Requirements.
Designers and developers should concern themselves with the total customer experience. Functional requirements refer to both what the system does and what the user does. *Task allocation* is the decision process through which activities are allocated to the computer and to the user. This step is deferred until after a task analysis has been done.

Functional requirements may be documented in a *functional specification*. The degree of formality for the functional specification varies greatly. Larger projects typically produce more formal and detailed specifications. The specification is often written in multiple levels starting with abstract (high-level) requirements (e.g., "the hotel management system should provide the capability to manage the allocation of rooms") down to very detailed (low-level) requirements (e.g., "a confirmation dialog must be provided to verify requests to delete a reservation").

Functional requirements are often constrained. For example, the client requesting the development of the hotel reservation system may specify that the existing hardware and operating system be used for running the new software. This requirement places limits on the type of offering we can design.

Functional requirements may be documented as a text document or as a dataflow diagram. (See Figure 4.2.)

FIGURE 4.2
Dataflow diagram for a hotel registration function. (Courtesy of IBM.)

FIGURE 4.3

Great products are based on real user requirements. (Reprinted with permission from United Feature Syndicate, Inc.)

Usability Requirements.   Usability requirements help the team to specify design objectives. The design can be evaluated against these objectives throughout the development process. Without explicitly specifying usability objectives, the desired performance levels will probably not be met. Through iterative design, usability measurements are compared against the goals, and the design is refined. Explicit requirements help designers to concentrate their efforts in areas where usability is most needed. (See Figure 4.3.)

Shneiderman (1998) recommended the following five types of usability requirements:

- Time to learn,
- Speed of performance,

- Rate of errors by users,
- Retention over time,
- Subjective satisfaction.

There are frequently tradeoffs among usability requirements. The relative priority of each requirement as rated by the customers themselves should be stated at the beginning of a project to aid in making these tradeoffs.

Each usability requirement should have a reason documented. For example, we may require that training time for a hotel management system be less than two hours because there is 50% annual turnover at the hotel and a system that requires more extensive training would not be cost effective. Documenting the reasons for usability requirements helps guard against establishing arbitrary requirements and is helpful in establishing the relative importance of a requirement when tradeoffs become necessary. It also has the benefit of getting new team members up to speed when joining a project.

Design objectives should be specified for each usability requirement. Specific criteria and methods of measurement should be provided. They may be specified as targets, minimum acceptable levels, and/or acceptable ranges. The measures are referred to as *usability metrics* and are detailed in a *usability specification*. Examples of usability metrics include completion time for specified tasks, number of errors per task, and time to complete each task. An example of a measurable usability requirement would be, "The top five user tasks will be performed 10% faster and with 10% higher satisfaction than the primary competitor, as measured in a usability lab test."

Figure 4.4 provides an example of a usability specification. Rather than measure usability as one global attribute for the product, it is convenient to break it down into many discrete attributes. The attributes are often based on user tasks. Based upon usability testing, one or more usability measures are collected for each attribute. The current level of user performance is specified along with the worst case and best case to show the degree of variance. These measures may come from a previous version of the product or may be left blank until data are collected. The planned level is the criterion you wish to obtain before the product is shipped.

Attribute	Measuring Method	Worst Case	Planned Level	Best Case	Current Level
Installability	Time to install	1 hour	30 minutes	10 minutes	Many can't install
Configuration	Success rate	0%	90%	100%	80%
Editing	Satisfaction	1	6	7	5

FIGURE 4.4
A sample row from a usability specification. (Adapted from Whiteside et al., 1988.)

Usability requirements are established through interviews with existing or prospective customers, task analysis, business needs, and competitive functions. Economic analyses are frequently done to determine whether development of a system meeting specifications will result in a net cost savings through increased efficiency, sales, better decision making, and the like.

A number of techniques have been developed for collecting and documenting user requirements. The Human Factors in Information Technology toolkit (Catterall et al., 1991) was designed to provide human factors input into the design of information systems. HUFIT consists of a number of tool sets. (See Figure 4.5.) The Planning, Analysis, and Specification (PAS) is designed to collect information about users' tasks and environments. The result of this analysis is a summary of user requirements and a functionality matrix. Data are initially gathered from all stakeholders in a project about the jobs they intend to do and the costs and benefits associated with the project. Customer, task, and environmental characteristics are then identified and described in the functionality matrix, which forms the basis of informed task allocation and evaluation. Tradeoffs are recorded in the Benefits and Costs columns of the PAS matrix. (See Figure 4.6.)

CASE STUDY: TOOLS FOR REQUIREMENTS GATHERING

- A survey is an appropriate tool for prioritizing user requirements.
- Design constraints do not obviate the need to understand customers' requirements.
- Quadrant charts help clarify and communicate design priorities.

At MetLife, one of the first activities prior to designing a new graphical front end to an existing system was to assemble a prioritized list of customer requirements

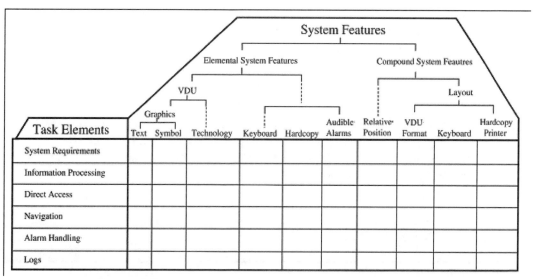

FIGURE 4.5
Example of the HUFIT functionality matrix. (Adapted from Preece et al., 1994.)

User Groups	Task Goals	Benefits	Costs
Desk clerks	Check available rooms	Faster access to availability information	Time to learn new system
Manager	Determine occupancy level	Better inventory control	Time to generate report

FIGURE 4.6
Example of a line from a PAS table. (Adapted from Preece et al., 1994.)

(Table 4.1). Even though we were largely constrained by the existing function of the system, we did have leeway both to add new task support and to change the organization and presentation of the existing task support objects on the screens. Surveys, focus groups, and roundtables had been conducted previously, so our first task was to organize and prioritize these data. The team first compiled a lengthy list of requirements (about 145) from all these data sources. The team went through each requirement, determining whether each had a direct impact on the end user (some of these were "under the covers" system requirements). The resulting subset of 38 user requirements was sent to end users in the form of a survey. We used five-point scales to measure frequency (how often this particular requirement arises), importance (how important the requirement is), and satisfaction (how satisfied users were with the current system's ability to meet the requirement) of each requirement. Results were compiled. Quadrant charts plotted importance plus frequency against satisfaction to determine "must meet" and "opportunity" targets for the new design.

Figure 4.7 is a sample of the data and the resulting quadrant chart. Each point on the chart was later labeled with the number of the requirement it represented. The quadrants were created by drawing lines through the means of both axes. The priority of each requirement was then labeled "HH" (high importance/frequency, high satisfaction), "HL" (high importance/frequency, low satisfaction), "LH" (low importance/frequency, high satisfaction), or "LL" (low importance/frequency, low satisfaction).

TABLE 4.1
Prioritized list of user requirements.

#	ImpFreq	Sat.	Prior.	Requirement
2	8.22	3.13	HH	Ability to locate key information without reviewing the entire claim (e.g., claim end date, benefit start date, etc.).
8	7.52	2.79	HH	New claims should be automatically identified and flagged.
11	7.37	2.66	HH	Plan Master provisions summary screen.
25	8.56	2.61	HH	Easy lookup for the Report #, Cov Code, Plan Code, Subcode Code, and SubPnt/CISCO Codes when creating a claim.
30	7.60	2.45	HH	New Claim Summary screen to display answers to common questions (e.g., last check date/amount, claim status, claim end reason code, etc.).
31	7.76	2.30	HH	Ability to see and print current payment and overpayment calculation details (e.g., FICA, FIT, SIT, LIT amounts; benefit amount by time period, etc.).

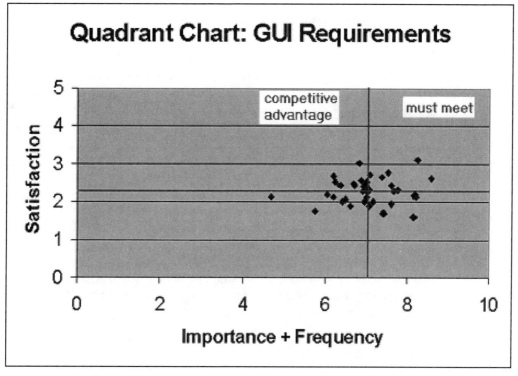

FIGURE 4.7
A quadrant chart—GUI requirements. (Courtesy of MetLife.)

Sizing and Scheduling

One of the more challenging aspects of UCD, as with all development efforts, is sizing and scheduling. At the start of a project, the team is asked to project required time and resources for the project. This exercise is especially challenging for new products because, with UCD, by definition, the team doesn't know the precise nature of the product that will ultimately be designed and developed. Only through the activities of UCD do they identify and have the product plan. However, most development management structures require early planning.

One of the techniques that satisfies the need for early planning is to start with a plan that is complete with regard to activities, but in which dates are tentative and then refined over time. One method is to use a template that describes the various phases of UCD and includes the entire range of UCD activities, adapting it for the particular project. Definite dates and resource needs are affixed to the earliest UCD activities. Later activities are presented with the approximate time and resources required. Then, as the project progresses, dates and resources are affixed to later activities.

The success of this approach requires that management trust the UCD team. Trust can be established first by hitting those early targets. If the team establishes a track record of timeliness, management is more likely to trust that later dates will also be met. Second, trust can be established by frequently updating the plan. As soon as the team is able, it should affix dates to the plan and communicate those dates to management. Third, management is more likely to trust the team if specific team members' names are affixed to the various activities. This gesture reflects the team's knowledge of what is to be done, who is most capable of doing it, and who will be responsible for its completion.

Creating the UCD Plan

The team should construct a plan for the UCD effort (Figure 4.8) including the various data-gathering and design methods that will be performed, who will perform them, and target dates for the activities. This plan is used to manage the UCD effort.

UCD Project Plan and Status

Offering	
Business segment	
Product description	
Competition	
Prime Competitor	
Users	
Primary	
Other	

Satisfaction	
Current offering	
Target	
Early ship	
Post ship	
Competition	
UCD	
UCD Team in place?	
UCD Team Lead	
Marketing	
Announce date	
Ease of use messages	
User Problems Fixed	
Severity 1	
Severity 2	
Severity 3	
User Hours	
Understand	
Evaluate	
Test	

FIGURE 4.8
UCD Project Plan and Status table. (Courtesy of IBM.)

Deciding which UCD activities to implement is not as simple as following a set of cookbook-like steps. Every UCD activity affords certain results, requires certain resources, and may carry certain risks if not undertaken. Furthermore, most UCD activities can be performed in a variety of ways; for example, requirements can be gathered by a survey, by observation, by interview, or by a group session. Each variation has strengths and weaknesses; some are more appropriate under certain circumstances. A thorough understanding of all the options and the implications of choosing them is required to plan a UCD effort.

CASE STUDY: KICKING OFF A UCD PROJECT

- A UCD plan template can help a team structure its UCD approach.
- Key activities for a team kickoff include providing education, assembling a team, and identifying the prime competitor.
- A design notebook that is accessible to all team members is essential, especially for geographically distributed teams.

A few years ago, we helped kick off the UCD efforts for a company that wanted to design a new systems management product. First, the team was assembled for UCD education. After attending courses in UCD basics and a UCD design workshop, it was time for the team to get busy. The team lead initiated several activities. Using a template distributed at the UCD class, the team progressed through a series of activities. In short, the team set out to customize UCD to meet the needs of its project. Here are some of the activities initiated by the team:

- **It examined and changed the composition of the team.** Representatives of key disciplines that hadn't been part of the team were added. These new members included a representative from the services and support discipline. A couple of the original members were moved from the core team to the extended team, the latter of which was also identified during this period.
- **It identified UCD activities essential to the product design effort.** The activities included the full complement of UCD methodologies: task analysis, competitive evaluation, design walkthrough, design evaluation and validation, early ship evaluation, and benchmark assessment.
- **It identified the target market.** The team concluded that there were two distinct market segments, characterized primarily by the types of networks the users managed: large and small to medium.
- **It wrote the audience description and recruiting criteria.** Criteria included, for example:

- "Does not use specialized systems management interface exclusively." (This criterion was intended to eliminate operators, system administrators, etc., from the pool.)
- "Is not exclusive to one technology (Jack of all trades)."
- "Systems management is not this person's official job, but it's what end-users come to this person for (the department guru)."

- **It identified competitors.** Because there were two market segments, the team needed to determine whether there were different competitors for each of these segments, which was indeed the case. The team identified potential prime competitor products.

- **It assembled a list of key design questions** to keep the team focused on the user and to help it identify the ease of use objectives. The team labeled this list, "Key Questions UCD Will Help to Answer." These questions included, for example:

  - "Should there be a common UI for both the A and B market segments?"
  - "What things do we need to focus on to be competitive in the A and B market segments?"

- **It set up a design notebook** to capture the team's UCD administrative information, user data, and design. The team created an intranet site that the team members could access from the home sites.

Concept Phase

After the team completes its planning, it then proceeds to the concept phase. During this phase, the team gathers additional data and sets forth the high-level direction of the new solution. All aspects of everything the customer sees, hears, and touches are designed at a conceptual level. For example, the marketing campaign is designed at a conceptual level. Decisions are made regarding the type of advertising media to be produced, where the ads will appear, and the key marketing messages that will be employed. The team decides service and support mechanisms (e.g., whether there will be free or fee access to service personnel and whether there will be web- or fax-based support). Packaging, sales channels, and other acquisition mechanisms are also determined, as are user assistance mechanisms (e.g., whether user assistance will be online or hardcopy). The high-level look and feel of the user interface is determined, and the user's conceptual model is designed. And, of course, the technology that drives the customer experience is determined.

During the conceptual design phase, the UCD team works together to form a unified vision for the new solution. Tradeoffs between aspects of the total customer experience must be made. For example, the user assistance objective of providing fully functional multimedia tutorials may be in conflict with a marketing objective of delivering a solution over the Web to users with low-speed modems. The team, by virtue of its multidisciplinary nature, is the proper vehicle for balancing conflicting design objectives.

The culmination of the conceptual design phase is the high-level design of everything the customer sees, hears, and touches.

Some or all of the following activities occur during the concept phase:

- Task analysis,
- Use cases,
- Contextual inquiry,
- Competitive evaluation,
- User profiles,
- OVID (Object, View, and Interaction Design),
- Prototyping,
- Design walkthrough.

Task Analysis

A wide variety of techniques are available for performing task analysis. These techniques all elicit descriptions of what people do and represent these activities in some useful form in the design of products. Although these techniques differ in their implementations, all the major techniques produce output that can be used for user interface design.

Task analysis has the following goals:

- To understand what the customer is trying to achieve (goals);
- To understand what the customer does (task procedures);
- To understand the environment in which the customer works (task context);
- To produce task descriptions;
- To create an abstract interaction design that focuses on how the customer will perform the tasks using the objects in the system, but without details of the UI design;
- To produce task scenarios that will be useful in design, prototyping, and evaluation.

Tasks are similar to the concept of function, but the two are distinct. *Functions* are activities, processes, or actions that are available in an application. *Tasks* are the sets of actions performed by a customer. In a hotel management system, one function is to maintain a table of room status (available, occupied, undergoing maintenance), and a related task is for the desk clerk to check room availability.

Tasks are groups of actions that together represent a meaningful operation. Pressing a key on the keyboard or moving the mouse does not constitute a task, but they are actions the customer may perform to complete a task.

The various task analysis techniques differ in their use of terminology. For example, "goal" and "task" are synonymous in some techniques, but they are defined quite differently in other techniques. For consistency, we have adopted the terms and definitions from Preece et al. (1994).

A *goal* is the state of a system the user wishes to achieve. For example, a goal of a desk clerk may be to check a customer into a room.

A *task* is the set of activities required, used, or believed to be necessary to achieve a goal. The goal of checking a customer into a room requires several tasks, such as checking room availability, checking for a reservation, and entering the customer's billing information.

An *action* is an operation the user performs to complete a task. The task of entering the customer's billing information will require a sequence of actions such as pressing keys on the keyboard, moving and clicking the mouse, and requesting information from the customer.

A *method* is a number of tasks or actions linked into a sequence. For example, we may provide keyboard-only or combined keyboard and mouse methods for performing the task of entering a customer's billing information.

An *object* is the focus of an action. In entering a customer's billing information, the customer and the data are objects.

We will describe the two techniques we use—hierarchical task analysis (HTA) and use case analysis.

Hierarchical Task Analysis.   Hierarchical task analysis is one of the best known forms of task analysis and has been in use for over 20 years. It begins with the collection of task scenarios and then creates graphical representations of high-level tasks broken into constituent subtasks and actions. HTA iteratively identifies tasks, categorizes them, and breaks them into subtasks. In each pass, the accuracy of the decomposition is verified. Shepard (1989) provided a complete description of HTA.

Information about tasks is collected from a variety of sources including conversations and other data-gathering activities with customers, observation of customers working, job descriptions, and operating manuals. One very efficient method of gathering tasks involves bringing groups of 20 customers per session to a Group Room and spending a full day articulating their current tasks and building a group-based common scenario model using a LAN-based groupware tool. Customers are also asked to specify the problems they are currently having carrying out their tasks and to react to how their tasks may change given particular product directions. At least one group session like this is carried out for each homogeneous user class.

A *task scenario* is an example of a task. It is a concrete instance with specific input and subtasks. A task scenario can be thought of as a test case. The task scenarios are documented as text descriptions. It is important to indicate who is performing each action (customer, system, etc.). The scenario looks much like a script for a scene in a play or movie.

Consider the following task scenario for the hotel management system.

Customer Check-In Scenario #1.

Customer: "I would like to check in. I have a reservation under the name Isensee."

Desk Clerk: "Let's see." Searches reservation list for the name Isensee.

System: Finds the reservation, returns customer information, assigns a room, and creates a key card.

Desk Clerk: "Here is your key card, Mr. Isensee. Your room is number 101."

Particular attention should be given to the most important tasks. The most important tasks are those tasks that are frequent or time or mission critical or where errors are significant.

Creating task scenarios for unusual circumstances is also helpful. You can elicit these scenarios by asking customers, "What is the most unusual request you have had in your job?" The system should not be designed specifically for these rare tasks, but it should be flexible enough to accommodate them.

Task scenarios should be expressed in terms of objects (nouns) and actions (verbs). It is helpful to express tasks in user language, which can help ensure that the customers will recognize system features as supporting the tasks they need to accomplish. Customer task language can be used in selecting and naming the task support objects in the system.

Task shortcut information should also be gathered. In each scenario, ask if there is a simpler, shorter, or more natural way to perform the task. This information can help the UCD team design easier ways to perform tasks that users may have already discovered.

Task scenarios are written for the way tasks are currently done and the way customers would like to be able to perform the tasks. Customers may not know of other, more efficient ways to perform their tasks. Designers may need to propose new task scenarios based on their knowledge of what is feasible.

Structure chart notation can be used to document the task flow. The specific task information from the task scenarios is abstracted into general descriptions of tasks. Descriptions should be brief and should be independent of the computer system and user interface. These descriptions should represent the ideal rather than the way tasks are currently conducted. The sequencing of activities is shown by ordering them left to right or top to bottom in the chart. Activities that may be repeated a number of times (iteration) are indicated by a small asterisk in the box. When one of a number of activities may be chosen (selection), a small circle is included in the box. A line in a box indicates the absence of an action. Figure 4.9 shows a chart for the goal of checking a customer into a hotel.

You can break tasks into subtasks until no further granularity is possible or until you have reached the level of detail you desire. If you stop too soon, you risk failing to identify some tasks. Continuing too far creates an overly complex task hierarchy and is not an effective use of time.

HTA can be described in three stages: starting, progressing, and finalizing.

- Starting the analysis
  - Specify the main task.
  - Break the main task into subtasks.
  - Draw out the subtasks, ensuring that they are logically and technically correct and that none is missing.
- Progressing the analysis
  - Decide the level of detail required and the point at which to stop the decomposition. For example, we could decompose the hotel customer check-in task down to the individual keystrokes, to the field

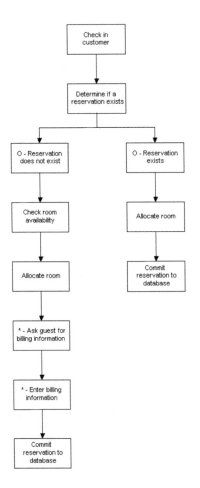

FIGURE 4.9
Example of an HTA chart. (Adapted from Preece et al., 1994.)

level (e.g., enter credit card number), or to the subtask level (e.g., enter all customer billing information).

- Decide whether to continue decomposing each task to the required depth (depth-first analysis) or to work on the next task (breadth-first analysis).
- The analysis continues until each task has been decomposed to the desired level.
- Finalizing the analysis
  - Check the analyses and generate all decomposition diagrams.
  - Check for consistency. It is good practice to present the analysis to someone who is not involved in it, but who knows the tasks well.

This process produces task models that represent the intended future structure of the tasks. For additional information on task analysis, see Hackos and Redish (1998).

Use Cases

Most object-oriented software design methodologies have adopted their own specific forms of task analysis. These analysis techniques include *use cases* (Jacobson, 1992, and Booch, 1994), *scenarios* (Wirfs-Brock et al., 1990, and Rumbaugh, 1991), and *scripts* (Rubin and Goldberg, 1992). Any of these techniques can be used to identify and document user requirements.

We will describe the use case technique because it is one of the most popular methods. For a more detailed description, see Jacobson (1992).

The use case defines the functionality the system should offer. It often serves as a contract for the system between the developer and the customer so nondesigners should be able to read it. The use case model defines the system from the customers' perspective. The model uses actors to represent the roles the users can play and use cases to represent what the customers should be able to do with the system. Each use case is a complete course of events in the system from the customers' perspective.

Determining Actors.   Actors are used to model the prospective users. The actor represents a user type or category (see Figure 4.10). When a customer does something, he or she acts as an occurrence of this type. One customer can instantiate (play the roles of) several different actors. Actors, thus, define roles that customers can play.

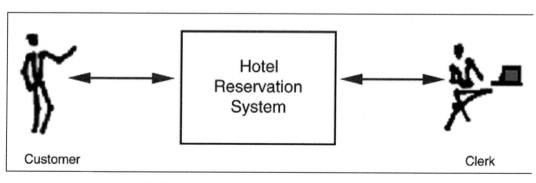

Customer   Clerk

FIGURE 4.10

The customer and the clerk are actors in the hotel reservation system. (Courtesy of IBM.)

The actors are used to model information exchange with the system. They can model customers or other systems that communicate with the system being designed. Actors constitute anything external to the system being designed. You can think of the actor as a class, that is, a description of behavior. The customer can play several roles, that is, serve as many actors.

Actors who use the system directly are called *primary actors*. (See Figure 4.10.) For example, the desk clerk is a primary actor in the hotel reservation system. Secondary actors exist so that the primary actors can use the system. Guests are secondary actors in the hotel system because they do not use the system directly. The clerk must collect information from the guest because, if the hotel had no guests, there would be no need for the system. Other systems may also be modeled as actors. For example, the hotel reservation system may request credit card account verification from another system as part of the check-in process.

Specifying Use Cases.   After we have defined what is outside our system, we can define the functionality inside it by specifying use cases. A use case is a complete set of events specifying the interaction that takes place between an actor and the system. The collected set of use cases specifies all the existing ways of using the system.

Actors are useful for finding use cases. Each actor will perform a number of use cases in the system. By going through all actors and defining everything they will be able to do with the system, we will define the complete functionality of the system.

Use cases are constructed through interviews with users where they are asked to describe the tasks they perform. The use case is a text description of these tasks. Nouns in the use case are underscored as potential objects in the system. The most significant objects are underlined and bold. (See Figure 4.11.)

> **Guests** make reservations with the **hotel**. The **hotel** will take as many reservations as it has **rooms** available. When **guests** arrive, they are processed by the registration clerk. The clerk will check the details provided by the **guests** with those that are already recorded. Sometimes **guests** do not make a reservation before they arrive. Some **guests** want to stay in nonsmoking rooms

FIGURE 4.11
Example of a use case.

Use case scenarios should describe how the customers will do their work when the new system is in place—not how the work is done now or what the problems are with how it is done today.

Use cases can be developed incrementally. You can focus on particular task areas, create individual use cases for each area, and then later join them to form the complete requirements model. This incrememtal development helps to break the work into manageable chunks and can also support parallel work by multiple analysts.

Weinschenk et al. (1997) recommended the following guidelines for creating effective use case scenarios.

- **Write from the user's point of view, not the system's point of view.** To match the way the customers should be doing their work, the scenario must be a list of user tasks. There is a tendency to start to describe what the system is going to do. If you really want a system description in your scenario, create a parallel scenario for the system.

- **Make sure you start with the customer's tasks.** To be able to use the scenario to create a conceptual model and the interface design, you must have a listing of customer tasks.

- **Include frequency information.** To create the most efficient interface design, you must document frequency of tasks in the scenario. If there are alternate paths, tasks, or decision points, you need to decide how frequently each path is to be taken. Will the customers be processing a new reservation most of the time or working with an existing reservation? This frequency information is critical if the scenario is to be most effective. What customers do most should be easiest to do. Your design decisions and tradeoffs come in large measure from this frequency information. For example, if your scenario indicates that working with an existing reservation occurs 80% of the time, then during design you would start the screen flow for that task with a list of existing reservations. If, however, your scenario indicates that starting a new reservation occurs 80% of the time, you would start the screen flow for that task with a blank reservation ready to be filled in.

- **Make note of critical tasks.** Criticality must be balanced against frequency.

- **Describe the future.** A scenario does not describe the customer's tasks now; instead, it describes the tasks they will perform when the new system is in place. Documenting the current tasks may tend to lead you to a design that is not much improved from the current system.

Contextual Inquiry

Contextual inquiry (Beyer and Holtzblatt, 1998) is a process for understanding customers and how they want to work on a daily basis. An interviewer conducts one-on-one interviews with customers in their workplace to understand their current work priorities, observes them as they work, and probes into actions as they occur. The interviewer strives to understand not just the tasks but also the customers' motivations and strategies for performing those tasks. Through ongoing discussion, the interviewer and customer develop a shared interpretation of the work.

The multidisciplinary UCD team then meets to hear the whole story of the interview and to draw and share insights relevant to the design. These sessions allow all team members to bring their unique perspective to the data and to share design implications from each of these perspectives. Through these discussions, the team raises issues and develops a shared understanding of the customers' work needs.

The team then draws a series of five work models that depict the work of individuals and organizations. The *flow model* depicts communication and coordination; the *cultural model* depicts culture and policy; the *sequence model* shows the detailed steps performed to accomplish a task; the *physical model* shows how the physical environment supports the work; and the *artifact model* shows how artifacts are used and structured in doing the work.

Next, the team uses consolidation to bring together the data from the individual customer interviews, enabling it to discover patterns and structure without maintaining the individual variation. The team then creates an affinity diagram, which consolidates issues and insights across all customers into a wall-sized hierarchical diagram. Consolidated work models compare each work model to the others to reveal common strategies and intentions, while retaining and organizing individual differences.

Finally, the team uses the affinity diagram and consolidated work models together to produce a single picture of the customer population the design will address. The design process uses these data to drive strategies for improving the customers' work by using technology to support the new work practice.

Competitive Evaluation

Very few products stand alone. To gain market share, your product must displace a competing product or an alternative way of doing things. Understanding the needs of your customers is necessary, but not sufficient, to build a successful product. You must also understand how your competitors are meeting those user needs and find ways to meet those needs better than your competitors do. For example, the Apple Newton was the first mass-market personal digital assistant (PDA). The US Robotics PalmPilot came along several years later but was far more successful because it better met customer requirements. The PalmPilot supported only a subset of the functions offered by the Newton, but these functions were designed to be easier to use and thus more useful to the customer. The PalmPilot also better met critical user requirements in areas such as physical size, battery life, and synchronization with desktop computers.

In traditional development processes, feature checklists are often used to compare a product with competitors. This comparison is based on the assumption that the product that offers the most features for the money will sell the best, but this assumption is often false. As shown in the PalmPilot example, a product with fewer features can often be much more successful.

Several methods for gathering competitive evaluation data include observation, surveys, trade press reviews, and lab studies. A competitive evaluation lab study is a method that analyzes in depth how user tasks are carried out today by the majority of the users in a given segment. A competitive evaluation can be a user study of a market-leading competitor product, or of an "analog" solution—that is, a nontechnology solution, in cases where the majority of customers don't use a computer solution today. Customers are brought into a UCD lab and perform a set of tasks using the competitor solution. The sessions are observed and logged by key members of the UCD team. Typical performance metrics are gathered, including time on task, number of errors and assists, competitor strengths and weaknesses, and satisfaction. For highly specialized products, expert users or instructors are often used in these evaluations. These sessions typically take half a day, but they could take longer depending on the product. The expert user performs typical tasks in addition to more specialized tasks using the competitor solution. The information captured includes quantitative measures such as user productivity as well as qualitative measures such as competitor strengths and weaknesses and satisfaction. Data gathered in a competitive evaluation are used to set competitive targets and benchmarks for the evolving design of the new solution.

CASE STUDY: COMPETITIVE EVALUATION OF SOCIAL INTERFACES

- If you can't find existing users, you can create them.
- Users may not just be individuals; they can be pairs of users, workgroups, peer groups, or even families.
- Techniques for competitive evaluation include real-world observation, interview, surveys, and traditional usability evaluation.

A few years ago, social interfaces were beginning to get some attention. The idea of creating a user interface environment resembling a real-world place (e.g., a room or office) instead of the familiar windows-based one was being explored by several software vendors. Examples of such interfaces included, at the time, the MagicCap PDA interface and Microsoft BOB (Figures 4.12 and 4.13). Around this time, we were working with a company that was exploring alternative social interfaces, which allowed users to choose from among several different realistic-looking places as their base user interface. When it came time to do a competitive analysis for this effort, MS-BOB was still a few weeks away from being commercially available. However, it was anticipated that BOB would be important in this particular domain. We decided that since there were no current users of this product, we would create some. Because BOB was apparently targeted at home users and was intended to be shared by those users, we recruited two families as our participants. We also hired an individual with a great deal of computer expertise to become a BOB "expert." When BOB hit the stores, we bought a copy for each family and for our expert user and asked them to use BOB for the next few weeks. We scheduled visits to the families' homes for a few weeks later. We observed them using BOB and interviewed them extensively on their experiences, likes, and dislikes. Our expert user performed a two-day in-depth evaluation in our UCD lab. During this time, he gave us a "tour" of BOB, showing us everything he had learned and comparing BOB to other systems he had used. All our participants completed questionnaires designed to measure BOB on several attributes. (See Figure 4.13.)

User Profiles

User profiles are detailed descriptions of the relevant characteristcs of each user category. Characteristics include descriptions of users' prior knowledge and experience; physical characteristics; social and physical environment; jobs, tasks, and requirements; and cognitive characteristics. User profiles classify the different types of users who will use the offering.

FIGURE 4.12
A screen from Microsoft's BOB. (Courtesy of Microsoft.)

OVID

Object, View, and Interaction Design is a method for designing the user interface by analyzing user goals and tasks and using these results to create an abstract diagram that describes the user model. The diagram, in conjunction with the visual specifications, enables implementation of the final design. An advantage of OVID is that the diagrams are readily understood by programmers and, therefore, can be translated into code design. OVID provides a common language for the multidisciplinary design team and implementers to communicate customer tasks.

One of the techniques employed in the OVID method is the identification of interface objects by underlining each of the nouns in the task analysis (see Figure 4.11) and by enumerating the tasks which were identified in the task analysis and list the functions which the system must provide to support each task.

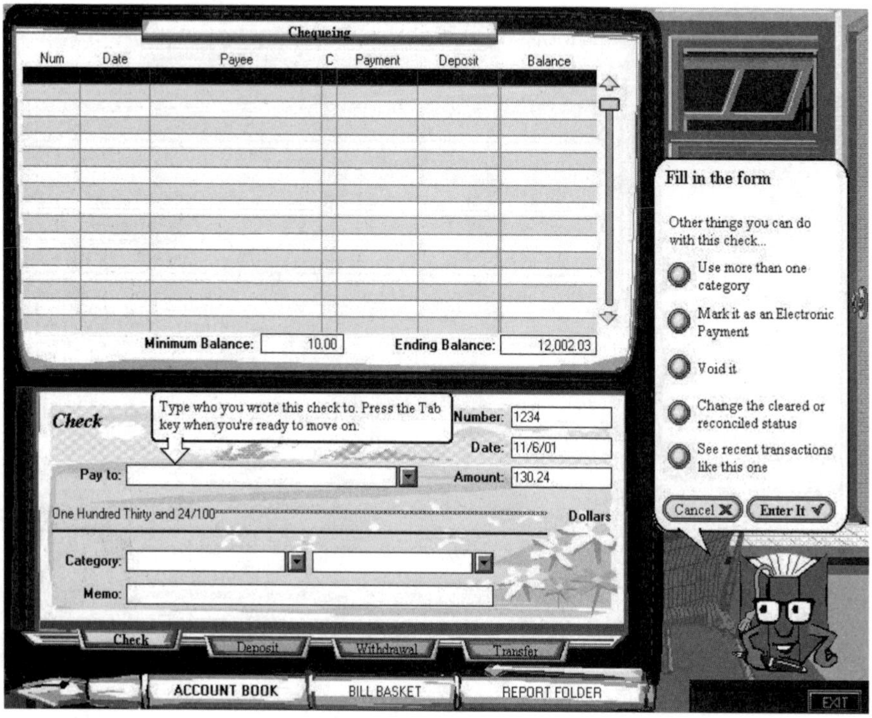

FIGURE 4.13
The Microsoft BOB Social Interface. (Courtesy of Microsoft.)

After the objects have been identified, the team depicts all possible states of objects and the transitions between these states in diagrams that represent object states and the transitions between states. Next, it identifies the views (the representation of an object) for each object and incorporates them as separate objects. The team then crafts the actual renderings. They use themes and metaphors based on their understanding of the user's goals, tasks, preferences, and the like as described in the user model. Next, the team associates views with tasks to ensure that each task is fully supported by appropriate views. The views are consolidated and checked for completeness in later stages of the design. Interaction methods for each view are specified next. An initial rendering of each view in each state is created using low- or high-fidelity prototyping (Figure 4.14). Finally, customers evaluate the prototypes. The object model and view designs are updated and retested until the design is ready for implementation.

For a detailed description of how to use the OVID method for user interface design, see the OVID methodology (Roberts, et al. 1998).

FIGURE 4.14
Detailed design of a view to support the hotel check-in task. (Courtesy of IBM.)

Prototyping

We often think of prototypes as representations of the user interface alone. But any aspect of a product that the customer sees, hears, and touches can be prototyped. For example, a magazine ad for a product can be prototyped as a pencil sketch of the advertisement. A few key marketing messages can appear; the rest of the content of the ad can be presented as "greeked" text until the actual marketing copy is written. A product box can be prototyped by pasting sketches of the proposed box top, sides, and back onto a box of the same dimensions that the proposed box will have. A tutorial can be story-boarded, and consist of major topics as well as greeked text. Even service and support mechanisms can be prototyped: Using a "wizard of oz" technique, a facilitator can mimic what a customer would hear when dialing a service number, for example, "Press 1 if you are a registered user. Press 2 if you wish to place a new order." The facilitator can even mimic what the customer will hear when on hold! There are many good reasons for prototyping, as we will discuss in this section. However, the primary reason for prototyping in the UCD approach is to gather user feedback to an evolving design. (See Figure 4.15 for a demonstration of the usefulness of feedback.) Let's now look at some reasons, techniques, and tools for prototyping.

Reasons to Prototype. Isensee and Rudd (1996) identified the major advantages of prototyping as

- Better collection of customer requirements,
- Cost saving,
- Increased quality,
- Evaluation of new interface techniques and functions,

FIGURE 4.15
Prototypes should be user driven, not technology driven. (Reprinted with permission from United Feature Syndicate, Inc.)

- Demonstration of feasibility,
- Sales tool,
- A clear specification,
- Early testing,
- Demonstration of early progress,
- Increased user satisfaction,
- A better design.

Using prototypes as an aid in customer requirements collection is particularly important in an iterative development methodology. Waterfall design methodologies require that the clients or end users have a clear idea of what they want a program to do and how they want it implemented, but users rarely have this level of understanding and vision. They just know that they have a problem and seek an expert to design a solution. Boar (1984) reported that 20 to 40% of all system problems can be traced to problems in the design process, and 60 to 80% can be traced to inaccurate requirements definitions. The cost to correct an error in a program increases dramatically as the life cycle progresses so it is critical to catch errors in requirements and design before coding starts.

Prototypes are used throughout the development cycle to verify customer requirements continually and to test that the product under development is meeting those requirements. Prototypes are very valuable as long as they are conducted in a disciplined requirements management process so that closure is assured.

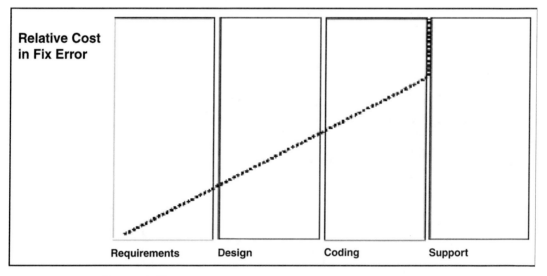

FIGURE 4.16
Graph of the increasing cost of fixing an error. (Adapted from Snyder, 1991.)

CASE STUDY: THE 3 × 3 METHOD FOR EXPLORING ALTERNATIVE METAPHORS

- Entertain alternative metaphors early in the design process.
- Test these alternatives with users.
- Test at least three metaphors, each to at least three screens deep.

While designing an automotive kiosk, we developed a method for evaluating the conceptual design of the kiosk user interface through customers' eyes. This method, called the 3 × 3 (Righi, 2001), allows designers to test and select from alternative metaphoric depictions of the user's conceptual model. The design team first gathers all requisite data for creating the conceptual model—customers' tasks and requirements and competitor information. Then the team brainstorms alternative ways of presenting the model. After paring down from several alternatives, the team selects the three best candidates for the 3 × 3 evaluation. The first three screens for each representation are sketched.

For the automotive kiosk, the abstract metaphor of an elevator was one of three chosen to depict the users' conceptual model. Vehicle shopping starts when the customer virtually enters one of the two elevators. (See Figures 4.17 and 4.18.) The elevator brings the user to the various floors of a showroom. Two elevators are available to allow users to shop either by brand or by vehicle type. Other metaphors tested included a road trip and a traditional showroom. (Figures 4.19.)

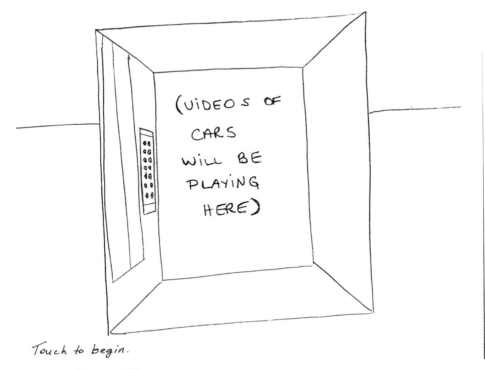

Touch to begin.

FIGURE 4.17
First of three screens of one of the alternative metaphors. (Adapted from Righi, 2001.)

We recruited three pairs of participants and engaged them in evaluation sessions. We showed the designs to them and had them work through the task of getting started at the kiosk. We watched and listened as they worked through the different metaphors. We attended primarily to how well the metaphors "fit" the customers' expectations: Were they meaningful? Did they enhance or detract from the usability of the screens? Real-time "tweaks" to the designs were made in an effort to strengthen each metaphor. The overall goal of this phase was to narrow the choices of model representations to one. After six participants tested the designs a clear preference—the road trip—was identified.

Low-Fidelity Prototypes. Low-fidelity prototypes are limited-function and limited-interaction prototypes. They are constructed to depict concepts and design alternatives rather than to model the customer's interaction with a system. Low-fidelity prototypes are constructed quickly and provide limited or no functionality. They are often built with paper and pencil.

Touch to select a floor to visit

FIGURE 4.18
Second of three screens of one of the alternative metaphors. (Adapted from Righi, 2001.)

Some people ask, "Doesn't it take almost as much work to build a proto-type as to make the final system?" The answer lies in Pareto's Law (Figure 4.20). It takes only a small amount of effort to produce much of what is wanted, but a large amount of additional effort is required to produce exactly what is wanted. It is generally possible to obtain a large amount of the most important capability of the system after implementing only a small part of the system. Effective prototyping requires that you determine and model only the key aspects of the system.

Users do not exercise a low-fidelity prototype to get a first-hand idea how it operates; rather, someone skilled at operating or explaining the prototype demonstrates low-fidelity prototypes. Low-fidelity prototypes are used early in the design cycle to show general conceptual approaches without much investment in development.

FIGURE 4.19
Third of three screens of one of the alternative metaphors. (Adapted from Righi, 2001.)

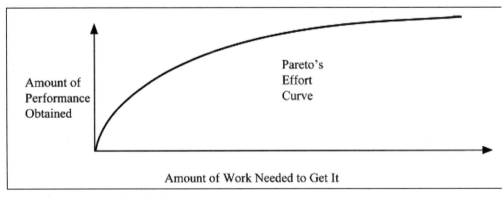

FIGURE 4.20
The curve of Pareto's Law. (Adapted from Nielsen and Mack, 1994.)

We like to use two forms of low-fidelity prototype for the user interface—abstract and concrete. Abstract prototypes serve as a communication vehicle between the human-computer interaction designer and visual designer. The designer's model is translated into views that are represented in an abstract form. For example, the following abstract prototype for the RealPhone represents the controls in block diagram form. The human-computer interaction designer can use this prototype to communicate the design to the rest of the team.

The visual designer works from the abstract prototype (Figure 4.21) and produces drawings of the interface as a concrete low-fidelity prototype (Figure 4.22). Users understand this level of prototype more easily than they understood the abstract version.

High-Fidelity Prototypes.   High-fidelity prototypes are fully interactive. (See Figure 4.23.) Using high-fidelity interface prototypes, users can enter data, respond to messages, open windows, and, in general, interact with the prototype just as they would a real application.

High-fidelity prototypes trade off speed of creation for accuracy. They are not as quick and easy to create as low-fidelity prototypes, but they faithfully represent what is to be implemented in the product. They can be made so realistic that the user cannot distinguish them from the actual product.

High-fidelity prototypes of the user interface are invaluable for usability testing. Even though low-fidelity prototypes address the layout and visuals of an interface (surface presentation), high-fidelity prototypes address the issues of navigation and flow. Users can operate the prototype as they would the real product. They can open windows and enter data. Messages are delivered at appropriate times. Data can be displayed in real time, and users can take action in response to the data. Errors and deviations from the expected path can be flagged and identified to the user as if using a real product. The customer can get a sense of how the product will operate and can make informed recommendations about how to improve the user interface.

CASE STUDY: REDESIGNING A FOOTBALL GAME USER INTERFACE

- Low-fidelity prototyping can be used for the design of new interfaces or for interface redesigns.
- Task flow modeling can be used to help accomplish one of the first steps in interface design: designing the user's conceptual model.
- Using familiar metaphors and presentation formats can make the interface more intuitive to its users.

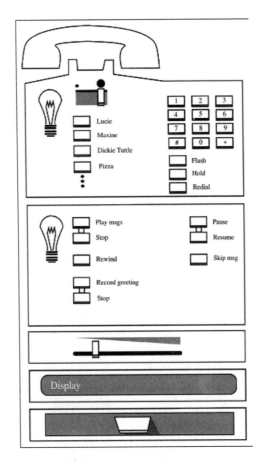

FIGURE 4.21
Example of an abstract low-fidelity prototype. (Courtesy of IBM.)

Designing a user interface is not a "one-shot" activity but rather an iterative process, during which all aspects of the interface are designed and tested. Conceptual design focuses on the user's conceptual model. As the design progresses, the UCD team can select and evaluate metaphors, determine screen layout, and design the look and feel. We use low-fidelity prototyping for all these design tasks, whether the project entails a redesign or a brand-new design. For example, on a project to redesign a football game interface, we used low-fidelity prototyping to design and test a new user's conceptual model. The game under redesign was packed with features and function. However, the existing interface showed the user almost all of this function on a single screen, with no apparent organization. (See Figures 4.24 and 4.25.) In short, the game did not have a coherent user's conceptual model.

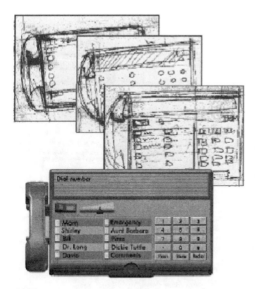

FIGURE 4.22
Example of a concrete, low-fidelity prototype—progressing from sketches to a three-dimensional model. (Courtesy of IBM.)

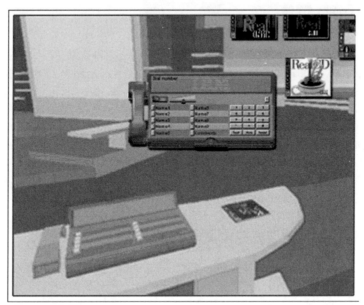

FIGURE 4.23
Example of a high-fidelity prototype—fully interactive. (Courtesy of IBM.)

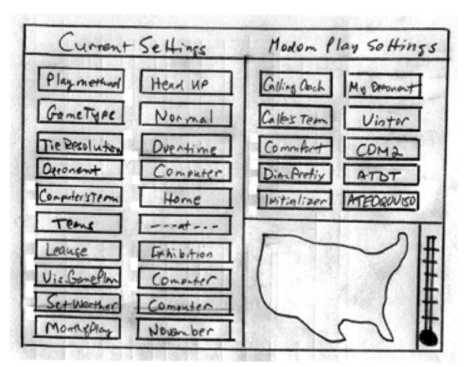

FIGURE 4.24
Original setup screen from football game.

To design the conceptual model, subject matter experts first performed a task flow modeling exercise. They sorted sticky notes, each containing a description of one of the user tasks supported by the existing game code, into "affinity groups." Then, they indicated the flow of these groups. We used these data to create low-fidelity prototypes of a proposed conceptual model. For example, the existing game allowed users to set many options before playing the game. The subject matter experts grouped these setup tasks into two categories—those related to league setup and those related to the current game to be played. Therefore, in our conceptual model design, we divided the options into two categories onscreen. We used familiar football terms as metaphors to represent this division of function; hence, the two sets of options were called Front Office and Field (Figure 4.26). We used other sports conventions to make the interface familiar to football fans. For example, in the existing interface, when two opposing team names were presented onscreen in the existing interface, they were presented side by side. However, on virtually all sports television broadcasts, teams are depicted top to bottom, with the bottom team representing the home team. Therefore, we proposed the latter presentation on all

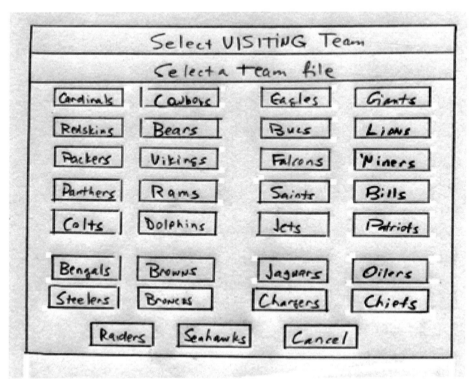

FIGURE 4.25
Original team setup screen from a football game interface.

screens and dialogs and in the documentation. We mocked up a variety of dialog boxes and other panels to communicate and test our new design ideas (Figure 4.27).

Comparison.   High- and low-fidelity prototypes each have their place in the development process. Both high- and low-fidelity prototypes have advantages and disadvantages. It is not a matter of choosing one or the other. You will typically implement both high- and low-fidelity prototypes on a project. Table 4.2 compares the advantages and disadvantages of each to help in choosing which is most appropriate for a given situation on your design project.

Managing Iteration.   The prototyping effort needs to be bounded. It can be tempting to continue revising the design and generating new prototypes without end. To be successful, the prototype must converge toward a better design at a reasonable rate of speed and cost. The goals of the proto-

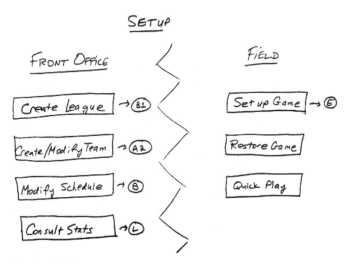

FIGURE 4.26
Conceptual prototype of new overall setup screen.

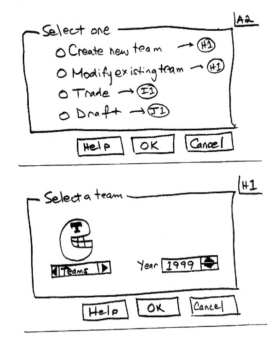

FIGURE 4.27
Dialog boxes for team setup.

TABLE 4.2
Comparison of high- and low-fidelity prototypes.

Low-Fidelity Prototype	
Advantages	**Disadvantages**
Lower development cost	Limited error checking
Evaluate multiple design concepts	Poorly detailed specification for coding
Useful communication vehicle	Facilitator driven
Address screen layout issues	Limited utility after requirements established
Useful for identifying market requirements	Limitations in usability testing
Proof of concept	Navigational and flow limitations

High-Fidelity Prototype	
Advantages	**Disadvantages**
High degree of functionality	More expensive to develop
Fully interactive	Time-consuming to create
User driven	Inefficient for proof-of-concept designs
Clearly defines navigational scheme	Not as effective for requirements gathering
Useful for exploration and testing	
Look and feel of final product	
A living specification	
Marketing and sales tool	

type can be specified in terms of usability measurements and goals. Progress toward those goals can be measured by usability tests.

Prototypes are not a replacement for up-front design work. Trying to iterate until you get it right without doing the up-front work not only is inefficient, but also can lead to uncontrolled iteration. Collins (1995) described several possible paths that iterative prototyping may take with respect to design goals. Figure 4.28 shows the ideal iterative process. This process assumes that there is an ideal solution in the space of possible designs and a

succession of prototypes spirals into it. By measuring the usability characteristics of the design at each iteration and modifying the prototype to address
problems, each iteration comes closer to the goal. Since unproductive iteration is avoided, time and cost are minimized.

Often, however, multiple designs are equally good. For certain features,
one design may be optimum. As you prototype other parts of the application, or add to the prototype, the optimum design may change. (See Figure
4.29.) These changes can cause the prototypes to wander unproductively
and perhaps never converge but can be avoided by prototyping the most
important (e.g., most critical, most frequently performed) functions first and
not significantly changing the design for less important functions. Another
strategy is to create a broad, horizontal prototype that represents most
aspects of the product.

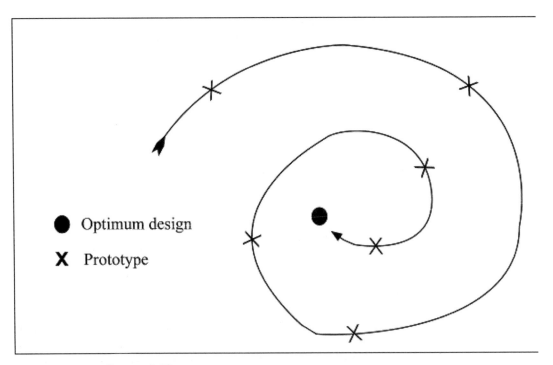

FIGURE 4.28
Idealized view of iterative design. (Adapted from Collins, 1995.)

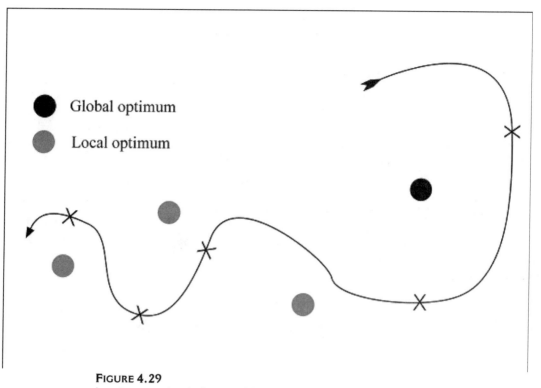

FIGURE 4.29
Iteration around multiple optimal designs. (Adapted from Collins, 1995.)

A prime cause of wandering iteration is not having a good conceptual model of the system, which forces developers to evaluate designs in a haphazard way. Trial and error is a very inefficient design technique.

Another potential problem with iteration occurs when designs circle the optimum without clear improvement. (See Figure 4.30.) Many alternative designs are prototyped, but no one can agree whether the new solution is better or worse. This situation typically arises when the project does not have usability goals and accurate measurements.

Design Walkthrough

A design walkthrough is a user-based competitive evaluation of the conceptual design of the total customer experience. A design walkthrough session is typically performed with groups of 20 participants per market segment and is held in a Group Room using a LAN-based groupware tool. The design walkthrough session normally takes one full day. Participants are

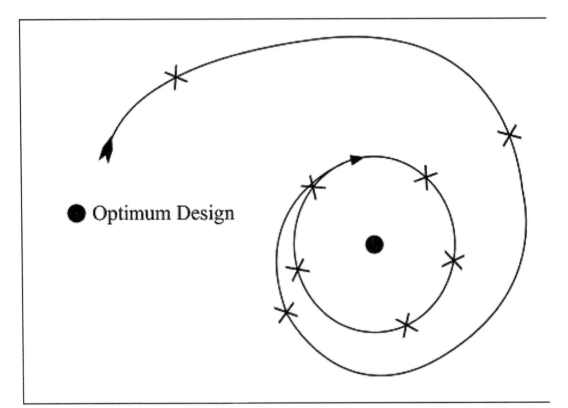

FIGURE 4.30
Iteration fails to converge. (Adapted from Collins, 1995.)

shown conceptual prototypes of the advertising, packaging, installation and setup, user interface, user assistance, and service and support. These elements are contrasted with the corresponding elements of the competitor's offering. Each element of the total customer experience design is evaluated using a standard online rating questionnaire and comment form, which yield comparative satisfaction ratings and customer ratings of design strengths and weaknesses.

Detailed Design and Development Phase _____

After the team has validated the conceptual design, the detailed design and development phase can begin. During this phase, the team designs and fleshes out all aspects of everything the customer sees, hears, and touches.

The content of the marketing materials is designed and implemented. Service and support details are specified, designed, and implemented. Packaging, ordering, and delivery mechanisms are designed and implemented. All aspects of the user interface are specified, including objects, behaviors, navigation, and interaction details. User assistance content is designed and produced. All aspects of the technology to support the total customer experience are designed and created.

Some or all of the following activities may occur during the detailed design and development phase:

- Prototyping,
- Heuristic evaluation,
- Usability walkthrough,
- Usability test,
- Design guideline development,
- Early-ship survey.

Prototyping

Prototyping activities, as described in the previous section, are employed in both the concept phase and the detailed design and development phase. During the concept phase, prototyping is used to arrive at a high-level design of all aspects of the total customer experience. Aspects of the product such as the user's conceptual model for the user interface, packaging concepts, and marketing ideas are explored, prototyped, and tested at a conceptual level. Low-fidelity prototypes are emphasized. During the detailed design and development phase, prototyping is used to work out all details of everything the customer sees, hears, and touches. For example, user interface screens and online help can be designed and tested. Low-fidelity prototypes are used extensively; however, high-fidelity prototypes are also employed to help flesh out the details of the design. Again, deciding which techniques to use and which aspects of the product to prototype during the concept phase vs. the detailed design and development phase requires a thorough understanding of the techniques.

Heuristic Evaluation

A heuristic evaluation is another method of examining a user interface design to determine the nature of usability problems with the intent of fixing those problems in an iterative design process. Heuristic evaluation entails multiple evaluators inspecting a user interface with regard to its compliance with a set of recognized usability principles, known as heuristics.

A heuristic evaluation provides a preliminary method for identifying potential usability problems, often at less cost than other evaluation methods. Consequently, it is often referred to as "Discount Usability Testing."

Various lists of heuristics can be used. One of the more popular has been proposed by Nielsen (1993):

- Visibility of System Status. The system should keep users informed about what is going on through appropriate and timely feedback.

- Match Between System and Real World. The system should speak the user's language, with words, phrases, and concepts familiar to the user, rather than system-oriented terms. Follow real-world conventions, making information appear in a natural and logical order.

- User Control and Freedom. Users control the task and system flow. However, users often choose system functions by mistake and will need a clearly marked emergency exit to leave the unwanted state without having to go through an extended dialog. Support undo and redo.

- Consistency and Standards. Users should not have to wonder whether different words, situations, visuals, interaction techniques, objects, or actions have the same meaning. Follow platform conventions.

- Error Prevention. Even better than a good error message is a careful design that prevents the error occurring.

- Recognition Rather than Recall. Make objects, actions, and options visible. The user should not have to remember information from one part of the dialog to another. Instructions for using the system should be visible or easily retrievable whenever appropriate.

- Flexibility and Efficiency of Use. Accelerators, unseen by the novice user, may often speed up the interaction for the expert user to such an extent that the system can cater to both inexperienced and experienced users. Allow users to tailor frequent actions.

- Aesthetics and Minimalist Design. Dialogs should not contain information that is irrelevant or rarely needed because it competes with the relevant units of information. This diminishes the relative usability of the relevant information.

- Error Recovery. Help users recognize, diagnose, and recover from errors. Error messages should be expressed in plain language (no codes), precisely indicate the problem, and constructively suggest a solution.

- Help and Documentation. Even though it is better if a system can be used without documentation, it may be necessary to provide help and documentation. Any such information should be easy to search, focus on the user's tasks, list concrete steps, and be a manageable size.

A weakness of heuristic evaluation is that it does not involve representative users. If it is the only activity undertaken, major usability problems will go unidentified. Also, problems identified by evaluators may not be experienced by users, thus leading the team to "fix what isn't broken" from the user's perspective. However, if users are unavailable to evaluate the design, heuristic evaluation can provide a direction for design improvement.

There are various techniques for conducting a heuristic evaluation:

- Evaluators can review an interface on a page-by-page or screen-by-screen basis and check the details of the page against each heuristic.
- Evaluators can find usability problems while reviewing an application, and then assign a heuristic to the problem.
- Different evaluators on the team can examine different aspects of the interface. A benefit of this method is that more of the offering is "covered" during the evaluation. A drawback is the loss of continuity; reviewers may not become familiar with the entire interface, leaving the consistency issues unidentified.
- Evaluators can try to complete various tasks using the prototype or application. Problems are noted in relation to the corresponding task.

Heuristic evaluation methodology is described in Nielsen and Mack (1994).

Usability Walkthrough

A usability walkthrough is an informal verification of the interface. (See Figure 4.31.) Nielsen and Mack (1994) describe several types of walkthroughs. In a walkthrough, evaluators step through a set of tasks to exercise the interface. They make sure that the interface works as designed and look for any obvious usability problems. Note that this is a different method than the UCD walkthrough mentioned earlier that deals with the entire customer experience in the conceptual design phase.

Usability Test

Formal usability testing is the most rigorous form of evaluation. (See Figure 4.32.) It typically employs experimental design methodology to measure user performance in a manner that allows statistical comparisons to be

FIGURE 4.31
Usability walkthrough. (Courtesy of IBM.)

FIGURE 4.32
Usability lab test. (Courtesy of IBM.)

made and conclusions to be drawn. Near the end of product development, lab test data can be compared to the usability goals as part of the benchmark assessment.

CASE STUDY: USABILITY LAB TEST OF A WEB SITE

- Usability testing can quickly uncover strengths and weaknesses of an interface.
- Problems and solutions must be specific to be useful to designers.
- Quick turnaround time of usability data is essential.

We recently performed a traditional lab-based usability test of a Web site for an Internet service provider (ISP). The primary objectives for the test were to determine whether users could easily find information about the ISP and whether users found the site attractive and pleasant to use. Fourteen users—including both current and potential future customers—were recruited as participants. A set of 17 information search tasks was compiled by sampling from the various Web pages. Participants were asked to think aloud as they worked. We recorded participants' behaviors, comments, task times, search paths, and errors. Posttest questionnaires to assess satisfaction were administered.

Because of the competitive nature of the information technology industry, and the brief "Web year," timeliness of reporting is an essential element of usability testing. The test sessions took place on Monday, Tuesday, and Wednesday evenings. The results were compiled, and a slide presentation of the results was created on Thursday. (See Figures 4.33 and 4.34.) The results were presented on Friday. The presentation highlighted the strengths and weaknesses of the site. To guide a redesign of the site, specific examples were given for each strength and weakness mentioned, and specific recommendations for improvement to both the high-level and low-level design were made.

Task satisfaction: Ease of completion

Task	Mean Curr	Fut
1. President and CEO	5.8	6.0
2. More about the company	4.2	5.9
3. Firewall info	5.8	6.2
4. Services for company's new hardware and software.	4.0	2.8
5. Visitors download which files	4.0	4.8
6. Press releases	6.5	6.0
7. Send info to your e-mail address	4.3	6.0
8. Open an account	6.5	4.5
9. Send your resume	5.0	6.5

1= Strongly Disagree, 7 = Strongly Agree

FIGURE 4.33
Results from a usability lab test.

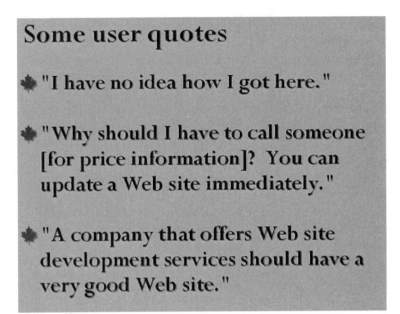

FIGURE 4.34
Results from a usability lab test.

How to Perform a Usability Lab Test.   This section covers only the basics of usability testing. For more comprehensive coverage, consult texts devoted to this topic such as Rubin (1994), Hackos and Redish (1998), Nielsen and Mack (1994), or Hix and Hartson (1993).

Designing the Test.   To perform a usability test, you must first decide the purpose of the test and then design an appropriate test. As in all testing, you must control the conditions and measure the results. Because control is critical, a usability lab is often employed (Figure 4.35). Decisions to be made when designing the test include

- Goals of the test,
- Number and description of test participants,
- Testing schedule,
- Testing method,
- Tasks to be performed,
- Measures to be collected,
- Data analysis techniques to be used,
- Methods for reporting the results and what actions to take based on these results.

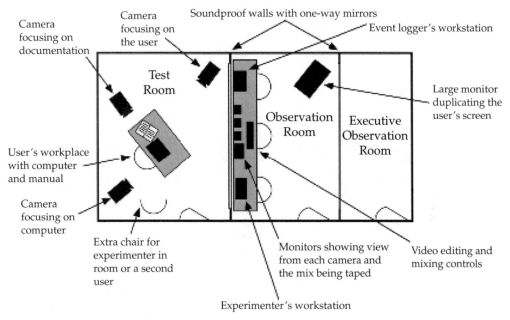

Camera focusing on documentation

Camera focusing on the user

Soundproof walls with one-way mirrors

Event logger's workstation

Test Room

Observation Room

Executive Observation Room

Large monitor duplicating the user's screen

User's workplace with computer and manual

Camera focusing on computer

Extra chair for experimenter in room or a second user

Monitors showing view from each camera and the mix being taped

Video editing and mixing controls

Experimenter's workstation

FIGURE 4.35
Floor plan of a typical usability laboratory. (Adapted from Nielsen, 1993.)

Selecting Participants. The type of participants you select depends on the purpose of the test. For example, if you are trying to predict performance in the general population, your sample should represent the population. On the other hand, if you are concerned about identifying problems that novice users may have using your product, then you should bring in novice users for the test.

You will typically want users who are knowledgeable in a particular domain. For example, an interface to be used by tellers in a bank should be tested on people with bank teller experience. Test participants without this domain knowledge may make errors that would not be likely to occur in a valid user population. Participants with the proper domain knowledge may be able to give you valuable suggestions on improving your product.

You will generally want a participant group with a mixture of skill levels. Novices may trip over problems that experts will breeze right past without noticing. Experts may find subtle problems (e.g., small inconsistencies and nonoptimum navigation) that novices would never notice.

The number of participants should be determined based on the analyses to be conducted. For statistical comparisons, power analysis is available to

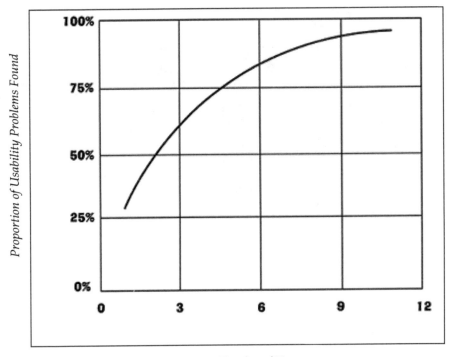

Number of Users

FIGURE 4.36
Graph of the number of core usability problems found. (Adapted from Nielsen and Mack, 1994.)

determine the number of subjects needed to find statistically significant results given certain values of key parameters (Cohen, 1988). Nielsen and Molich (1990) found the optimum number of participants to be three to five per user class. Smaller samples missed problems or were too heavily influenced by a single, deviant participant, and larger number may not be worth the diminishing returns obtained.

Figure 4.36 shows the curve of diminishing returns in proportion of problems identified as sample size increases.

Landauer (1996) graphed the cost–benefit ratio of usability testing as the number of tests or number of evaluators increases. (See Figure 4.37.)

You may occasionally want to use participants for more than one test condition or for repetitions of a given test. This approach may increase test efficiency, but it introduces potential biases.

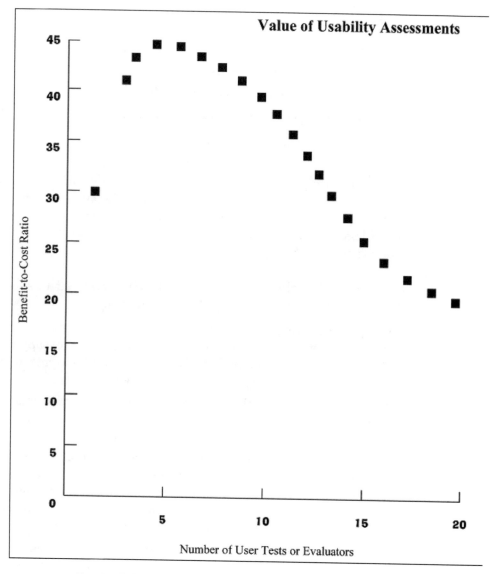

FIGURE 4.37
Benefit-to-cost ratio of usability testing. (Adapted from Landauer, 1996.)

Developing Tasks.   A set of benchmark tasks, drawn from earlier task analysis activities, should be developed to compare user performance to the goals that have been set for the project. Other representative tasks are added to ensure that all important functions and areas of the application are

> 1. Record a reservation
>
> 2. Check in a customer
>
> 3. View a room-cleaning list
>
> 4. Generate a day-end financial report

FIGURE 4.38
Some sample tasks for the hotel reservation system.

evaluated. In early phases of the development cycle, the task list may be short, exercising only the functions available in the prototype at the time or those that are most frequent or important. In the later stages of development, the task list must be comprehensive enough to evaluate all significant areas of the product. (See Figure 4.38.)

Preparing Materials.   Materials need to be developed to support the test. These materials may include the following elements:

- **The prototype.** You must have some form of prototype of the system for the participants to operate. The prototype must be capable of supporting the scenarios you are interested in testing. You may need to enter particular data into the prototype and reset it after each participant.

- **Background questionnaire.** The background of the participants may influence their performance. It is important to have a questionnaire to collect this data so that it can be used in later analyses.

- **Test facilitator instructions.** You should carefully list all the steps the test facilitator should perform during the test. You want to make sure that you don't forget any steps in the rush of running the test, and you want the procedure to be consistent from one participant to the next. You may have assistants who need to follow the same procedure.

- **Participant instructions.** Participants should be given enough information to understand what tasks they should perform, but not so much that you lead them toward a particular way of performing the task. In general, these instructions should be expressed in terms of goals rather than procedures.

- **Data collection forms.** Your data collection forms should be tailored to the data you want to collect so that you can record results as quickly as possible without making errors or losing track of what the participant is doing. Significant events often happen quickly and one after another. Many labs use data-logging software that can collect and then summarize the data. It may also be synchronized with video to allow you to return to view significant events from the test easily.

- **Video and audio taping equipment.** Recording the test is often helpful. If the test facilitator misses something in real time, she can go back to the tape to review the event. Video summaries also can be very persuasive in convincing people who were not at the test that a problem exists. Typically, at least two cameras are used—one to capture what happens on the screen and the other to capture participant actions.

- **Confidentiality and permission forms.** If you don't want test participants to talk about your product outside the company, you need to warn them that the information is confidential and have them sign a form agreeing to their silence. You should also ask them to sign a form acknowledging that they are aware that they are being recording and allowing you to use these recordings and other results of the test in your report.

- **Posttest interview list.** Prepare a list of questions to ask and points to go over at the end of the test. You may want to ask their opinion on the product and specific aspects of it, ask questions about some of their actions in the test, and ask them to clarify comments they made during the test.

Data Collection. You should control test conditions as carefully as possible to prevent such extraneous effects as differences in instructions or stimuli to influence the results. Consequently, a uniform set of introductory remarks should be delivered to participants. These instructions typically state that the purpose of the session is to evaluate the system, not the participants.

Common measures for a usability test include task time, errors, assists, and satisfaction. The performance measures can be collected through observation or by instrumenting the prototype. Data-logging programs are available for entry and classification of data.

Tests are often videotaped to allow the test facilitator and others the opportunity to review events that happen quickly and may not be adequately understood or documented in real time. An edited video is often very persuasive evidence when reviewing test results with development team members who were not present during testing. The video usually includes an audio record of the testing, which is known as a *verbal protocol*

(Ericsson and Simon, 1985). A verbal protocol provides a wide range of information such as the way a participant plans to do a particular task, identifies interface objects, and understands the messages. This audio information captures subtle cues such as comments or tone of voice that aren't captured in other measurements and which can provide important clues in understanding the reasons behind participant actions.

A form of verbal protocol frequently used is a *think-aloud protocol*. Participants are asked to say out loud what they are thinking as they perform a task. This protocol is very helpful in understanding the reasons for participant errors. A drawback is that it is difficult for participants to talk while performing the task without distracting themselves and consequently having a negative impact on task performance.

Interviews and questionnaires are used to collect information about the background and experience level of test participants. They can also be helpful after a test to elicit participants' comments about the design and additional information needed to understand why the participants did what they did during the test.

Data Analysis.   Statistical data analysis techniques are recommended whenever you have sufficient sample size and quantitative data. These techniques allow you to judge which effects are statistically significant or statistically powerful vs. those that are so weak that they may be attributable to chance variations. Comparisons may be made against benchmark goals, between competing products, or between design alternatives.

Whether the test is large or small, the amount of data collected in a usability test can seem overwhelming. It helps to organize the analysis into steps and proceed methodically so that each piece is of a manageable size and so that you don't miss anything. One way to segment the information is to look at the data from one task at a time. Focus on identifying problems first and then go back and develop solutions.

Results are commonly delivered in a report listing the problems, frequency of occurrence, severity, and recommended solutions. Time on tasks, errors, assists, satisfaction, and any other measures you have collected can be compared against the usability goals you have set. The report is often supplemented with a videotape documenting significant events in the testing.

Design Guideline Development.   In order to document and communicate a design, a UCD team may choose to write a design guideline document, or "Spec." This document lays out all of the details of the design and serves as the blueprint for the offering. It is written at a very low level of detail and includes elements such as the following:

- Visual specifications (e.g., font type and size)
- Interaction specifications (e.g., what will occur at the click of a control)
- Error conditions
- Associated messages
- Selection states (e.g., selected, rollover, not selected) and their visual appearance

The document ensures consistent look and feel across the offering.

Early-Ship Evaluation

An early ship evaluation, also known as a beta evaluation for software products, occurs just prior to a product's release. A prerelease version of the entire product (including the packaging, advertising, hardware, and code) is provided to representative users who have been recruited as participants. Information is collected directly from these participants, who use the product in their real-world setting, through the use of surveys and usage instrumentation. The information collected includes customer satisfaction, problems experienced, and a tracking of use of particular parts of the product. Data are collected in phases including initial install, early use, and more prolonged use. The last installment is particularly important given that it is usually not possible to assess extended use in the laboratory.

Life-Cycle Management Phase

UCD is a full-cycle from product inception, to product design, to development and deployment. As such, even after the product is released, UCD is employed to ensure the product has met its objectives and will meet the needs of its intended customers. Further, data gathered during lifecycle management can be employed to improve the follow-on version of the product.

Customer Satisfaction Survey

Customer satisfaction is an expression of perceived value of a product. A customer satisfaction survey describes the degree to which a customer is satisfied with the level of service received and/or the ability of a given tool or product to meet stated and unstated business requirements.

CASE STUDY: CUSTOMER SATISFACTION

- Measure satisfaction of both internal and external customers.
- Realize it is never too late to improve the total customer experience.
- Ask for comments to elaborate on satisfaction measures.

BMC Software was developing a product that reported on the performance of e-business Web sites. The product was being developed without following a UCD process. Well into development, the programming team realized that the user interface was not well designed and would be too difficult for customers to use. The usability and user interface design team was contacted to fix the problems. The usability specialist quickly identified the major problems as an interface focused on product features rather than the tasks the customers perform, an overly complex network install, and no indication where the user should start when the product first comes up.

These problems were addressed by the redesign (Figure 4.39) of the UI and the addition of a Product Launcher (Figure 4.40) which guides the user through the installation and configuration process.

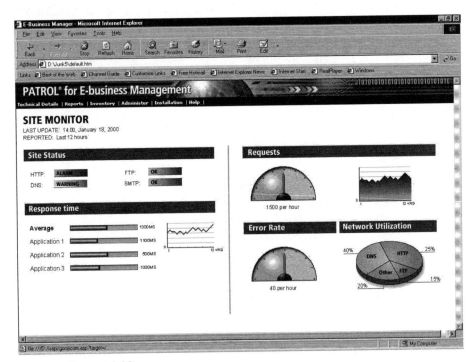

FIGURE 4.39
Redesigned user interface. (Courtesy of BMC Software.)

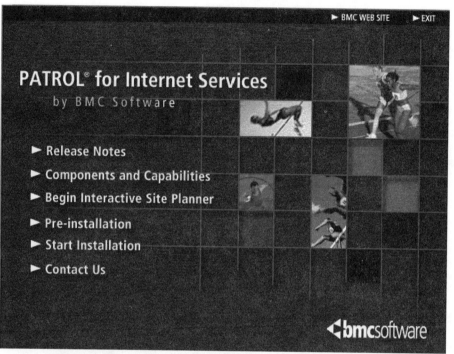

FIGURE 4.40
Product Launcher. (Courtesy of BMC Software.)

The redesign was shown to all members of the development and marketing teams, industry analysts, and customers. Comments included:

- Several of the analysts who are typically very critical were truly blown away and impressed by our new UI.—Tech Lead
- Gee, what else can one say but WOW!!—VP of Development
- We have managed to put together a fairly compelling user interface for our product in about 3 weeks time! This is amazing.—Program Manager
- This is awesome!!! ... it is absolutely a deal clincher.—Marketing Manager

Although it was not possible to follow the complete UCD process throughout development of this product, doing what was feasible toward the end still had a tremendous impact. As a result, the development team got the UCD "religion" and adopted UCD early in the next product cycle.

Benchmark Assessment

During the final stages of the development cycle, you may want to carry out a benchmark assessment, comparing the final product with the competitor on the core tasks identified during the early stages of the project design. This assessment includes the usual core quantitative measures such as time on task, number of assists, number of errors, and qualitative measures such as customer satisfaction.

Postmortem Evaluation

Postmortem evaluations are often held to review the reasons for success or failure of a project. They help to determine how the process can be improved in the future. Key members of the development team conduct the postmortem review. A moderator who was not part of the project often runs the postmortem. This review is often supplemented by post-ship data that measures performance of the product in the field.

Optimizing Your Implementation of the Approach

Authors' note: Many of the tools described in this chapter are available either for free or for a fee from their respective developers. IBM tries to make many of its tools available externally on its Web site and will continue to do so in the future. Other IBM tools described are for internal use at IBM at this time, but they provide ideas for tools that you could develop for your company.

The previous chapters provided an introduction to our Integrated User-Centered Design approach, discussed how to implement it in an organization, and outlined the deployment of UCD on projects. This chapter explores the various ways in which UCD can be further optimized with the application of advanced technologies as well as advanced methods and techniques.

Many UCD methods can be heavily labor intensive, and it often takes too much effort to efficiently collect customer information. Technology is underutilized in typical UCD methods. Adding to the amount of time required for proper design is the ever-increasing need to ensure that products are "internationalized" for the world marketplace and are tested in a context-rich environment yielding greater ecological validity of results. Finally, multidisciplinary teamwork, a critical ingredient to great design, is difficult and requires strong coordination and teamwork.

Despite the increase in focus on ease of use and usability within the industry (Mao, Vredenburg, Smith, and Cary, 2001), many product teams still forgo involving customers in the design and evaluation of their products because acquiring ready access to representative customers and the lack of rapid turn-around techniques to get customer input is difficult. In fact, even groups who have embraced UCD in the past are finding it increasingly difficult to involve customers given ever-decreasing development cycles, or the new so-called " Web-year" phenomenon.

To address these varied challenges, some companies used various tools and technologies. The applications include enhanced methods for getting teams aware, trained, and up and running; methods for recruiting customers for UCD studies; tools for capturing user information (largely using the Internet); and tools for information sharing across design teams, practitioner teams, and management teams companywide.

Education, Performance Support, Organizational Learning

As discussed in Chapter 3, introducing UCD to an organization is often the most challenging aspect of the overall experience. Technologies can be effectively used to optimize this process. In addition to the traditional overview presentations and classroom education, newcomers to UCD can also be directed to brief online videos that show "UCD in action." The CD that accompanies this book contains a 10-minute overview audio-video file as well as several 1- to 2-minute video segments on specific topics. (See Figure 5.1.)

FIGURE 5.1
Screen from a video of UCD in action. (Courtesy of IBM.)

These videos are often a great first introduction to UCD. The longest video only takes 10 minutes, and who doesn't have at least that much time to spend on this topic? This introduction is often the first "hook" for newcomers. These "UCD in Action" video segments can effectively communicate the essence of an aspect of UCD in a couple of minutes that only a guided tour of a UCD laboratory could accomplish in several hours. What task analysis involves, for example, can be very quickly illustrated with a video (see Figure 5.1) in a way that presentations and documents cannot accomplish.

After viewing the videos, people are often interested in more in-depth information about the approach. Textual material about UCD is most appropriate for this study and can be made available on an intranet Web site. Both introductory material and performance support information can be made available in this way. The latter is typically most effective if shown in a step-by-step wizard interface. Figure 5.2 illustrates the Web site used at IBM for this purpose.

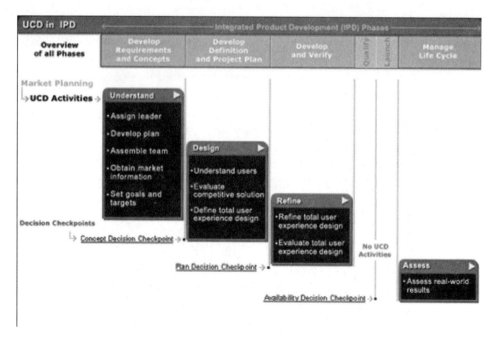

FIGURE 5.2
Web site with UCD information. (Courtesy of IBM.)

Both introductory and performance support information must be written in such a way as to be directly relevant to your organization. If your organization has a business checkpoint process in place, then the UCD information should be shown within the checkpoint structure. If your organization has a less formal approach to business and/or development processes, then the UCD information should be characterized in the same format. In other words, you should design your online UCD intranet information using UCD principles to ensure that the design is customized appropriately for the user. Guard against simply taking a UCD process document, exporting it to HTML, and then placing it on your intranet Web site. You should ensure that the information is both engaging and informative. This step is especially necessary with UCD information because many of the engineers in your company may not be motivated to read such material. Therefore, the material must be that much more compelling compared with virtually any other topic in order to get noticed and read.

Assistance for carrying out specific methods of UCD can also be effectively delivered to a remote team of practitioners via an online education webcast. This approach is a good way to make the information come alive. An expert on the method or tool provides an overview and demonstration of it and gives remote attendees an opportunity to gain some hands-on experience with it via an exercise. The session concludes with a question-and-answer period.

It is often also effective to make experts on particular methods and tools available to others in the company by providing practitioners a file of names together with their expertise for inclusion in your company's instant messenger software. When people in the company have quick questions about their project, they can send a message to the expert for advice directly. Experts can also set their messaging client software so that they are available at certain times and not available at other times. This practice will prevent messaging from interrupting the experts when they are doing heads-down work. See Figure 5.3 for an example of this type of approach.

An additional or alternative way of encouraging cross-company discussion on UCD topics involves making a discussion database available to all employees. This database can be used to disseminate the experience of your experts, collaborate on solutions to design issues, and capture organizational knowledge. With regard to the latter, new employees should be encouraged to read through the UCD discussion database to see if a particular item has already been addressed there before asking a question. (See Figure 5.4.)

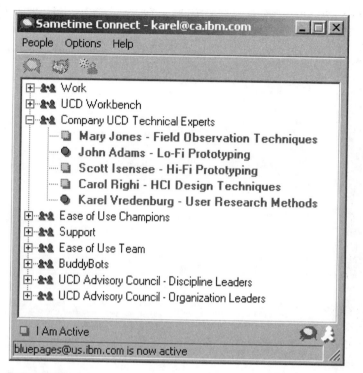

FIGURE 5.3
List of UCD experts in an instant messaging session. (Courtesy of IBM.)

Lastly, if in-person communication is impractical, Webcast software can also be used to update the companywide team on key developments, strategies, new techniques, and demonstration successes and to discuss issues. Many varied methods of communication are typically required to introduce and subsequently deploy and further optimize UCD in an organization. All these elements are part of the overall communication strategy depicted in Figure 5.5.

All the information and tools can also be presented on a central company Web site so that practitioners and others in the company can access it from a single intranet location. Practitioner tools and information for UCD teams and management at IBM are available on an intranet Web site called the UCD Workbench. (See Figure 5.6.)

The UCD Workbench can become a critical ingredient of UCD by enabling:

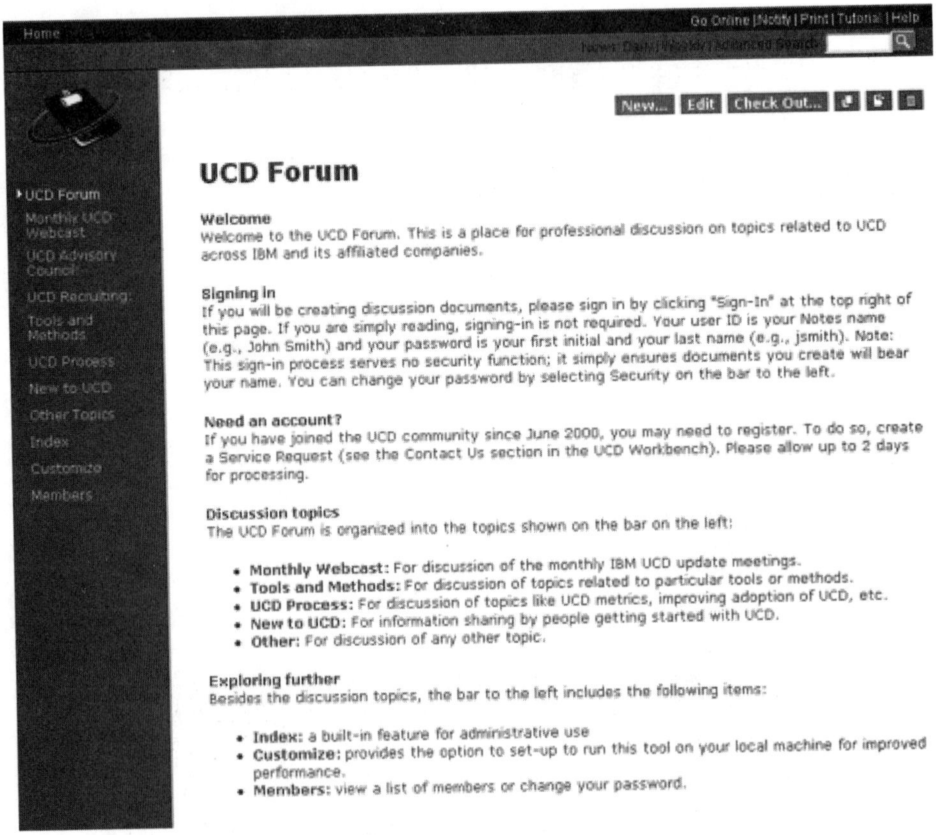

FIGURE 5.4
UCD discussion database. (Courtesy of IBM.)

- Communication to and collaboration among the companywide practitioner team;
- Capture and sharing of UCD best practices, intellectual capital, and organizational learning;
- UCD knowledge management, skill acquisition, and enhancement;
- Enabling tools to optimize carrying out UCD including a global audience;
- A mechanism for the companywide tracking and management of UCD metrics and progress.

At IBM, the UCD Workbench has focused on the following major features:

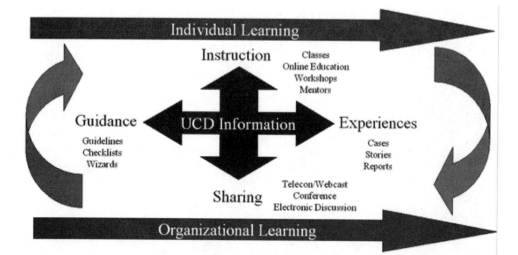

FIGURE 5.5
Communication strategy. (Courtesy of IBM.)

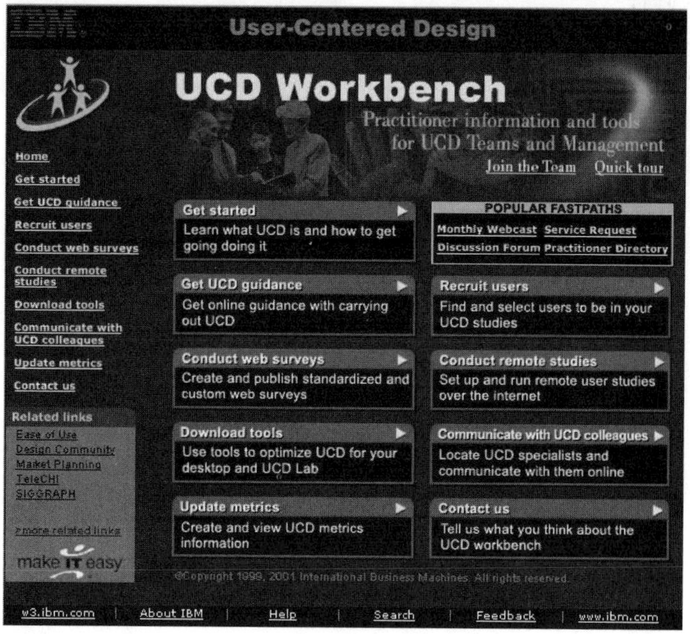

FIGURE 5.6
UCD Workbench. (Courtesy of IBM.)

- **Ease of use.** The UCD Workbench offers an overall design that features a task-based single source of practitioner information and tools for UCD teams and management. A quick tour and several Web-based wizards help users get oriented with the Workbench and carry out key tasks with it. Popular fastpaths further minimize clicks to get to frequently accessed parts of the Workbench.

- **UCD guidance.** If practitioners need advice on getting an organization started with UCD or carrying out specific parts of the process, the UCD Workbench has "getting started" and expert-level information on the process, methods, and tools including streaming video overviews. Practical advice for both novices and experts from the IBM experts is included.

- **Task optimization.** The UCD Workbench includes tools to support the key tasks UCD practitioners carry out. These tools help with recruiting participants, conducting Web surveys, running remote studies, capturing project information, logging customer sessions, analyzing user information, and sharing previous studies with colleagues in a survey library.

- **Team communication.** If practitioners want to keep up with the latest research on UCD-related topics, need to find a UCD contact in a particular division, or want to discuss a UCD-related issue with other members of the internal or external community of UCD professionals, the Workbench includes support for this type of cross-company UCD practitioner communication, including UCD Webcasts, an instant messaging list of discipline and division UCD leaders, a directory of cross-company specialists, and internal and external online practitioner discussion forums. These forums support rich text and images and can also be downloaded and used disconnected on your desktop.

The Workbench is the portal through which all relevant IBM UCD cross-company information passes. Importantly, it is also includes all deliverables from the UCD Advisory Council and Integrated Product Development (IPD) UCD process information for all groups and divisions of the company: hardware, software, and services. Without the UCD Workbench, individual lab and geography skill groups would be isolated and would not gain the benefit of the organizational learning and best practices from across the company. They would carry out UCD in a suboptimal manner requiring more resources and not addressing the worldwide audience of customers unless they developed their own tools for such things as remote testing and Web surveying, and would feel less a part of a vibrant community of practitioners at IBM.

The UCD Workbench is regularly featured in industry workshops at major professional conferences as a model of enabling a companywide UCD team in a large corporation. Particular tools within the UCD Workbench are given as examples in the following sections.

Multidisciplinary Communication and Collaboration __

Making good multidiscipinary design happen can often be a challenge. Chapter 3 observed that many of the disciplines that need to work together to design the total customer experience often have not done so in the past. In fact, many are in different parts of the company and sometimes different parts of the globe. One way to address these changes is to bring multidisciplinary team members together electronically. In that way, all members share a common virtual space whether they are from a department down the hall or from a team several time zones away. A groupware database tool can be very effective in this instance.

IBM developed a UCD RealTime tool, which is a Lotus Notes application (Figure 5.7). It can be used to capture key information about team members, including their addresses, phone numbers, roles, and responsi-

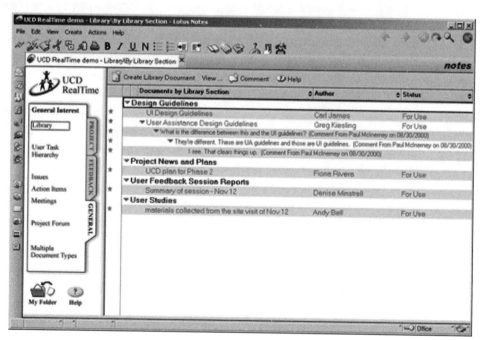

FIGURE 5.7
UCD RealTime. (Courtesy of IBM.)

bilities. It is organized around key customer task information that all design should be based on. All other information captured is cross-referenced with this central task information. All schedule, plan, action item, problem, and report information is captured. Design artifact descriptions and images are stored together with customer feedback information. There is also a facility that encourages electronic discussion of ideas on the team. Even members of the team who are traveling can keep up with the team's work by using the tool's replication capability. The experiences of teams who have used tools like this have been extremely positive, reinforcing the need to introduce a virtual environment to promote effective multidisciplinary teamwork.

Recruiting Participants

A time-consuming activity for most organizations is the recruiting of appropriate study participants. UCD, when conducted properly, requires a lot of customer participants. The challenge is then to find sufficient numbers of representative customers for the many user sessions UCD involves. Many organizations get through the early stages of making an organization aware of the need to do UCD, do the requisite education, and hire appropriate staff only to find an entire organization primed and skilled to start doing UCD but not having any participants with which to carry out the specified UCD activities. The appropriate application of technology can effectively address this problem.

This technology can include a Web-based recruiting survey on an external Web site (see Figure 5.8) together with appropriate incentives to participate such as "Win a Notebook Computer" and regular advertisements in news groups for the markets served by the company. This approach has proven to be a highly successful way to recruit participants for many projects. Product registration information can also be captured into a database for customers who have indicated that they are willing to be contacted. Practitioners across the company can query both of these databases by accessing an intranet Web site. Using these recruiting tools can dramatically increase the ability of development teams to get to their users quickly and worldwide. Practical experiences and recent privacy legislation should also be taken into account, however, when using these approaches.

Participant Recruiting Database

The participant recruiting database is composed of a demographics and product usage survey on the Internet, a central relational database, and a Web query interface on the intranet. Potential participants complete the Web-based form asking them such information as name, address, e-mail address, characteristics of their computer use, and information about the specific products they use and their proficiency at using them. It also asks the type of studies for which they would like to be considered—Web survey, telephone interview, on-location study, and so on.

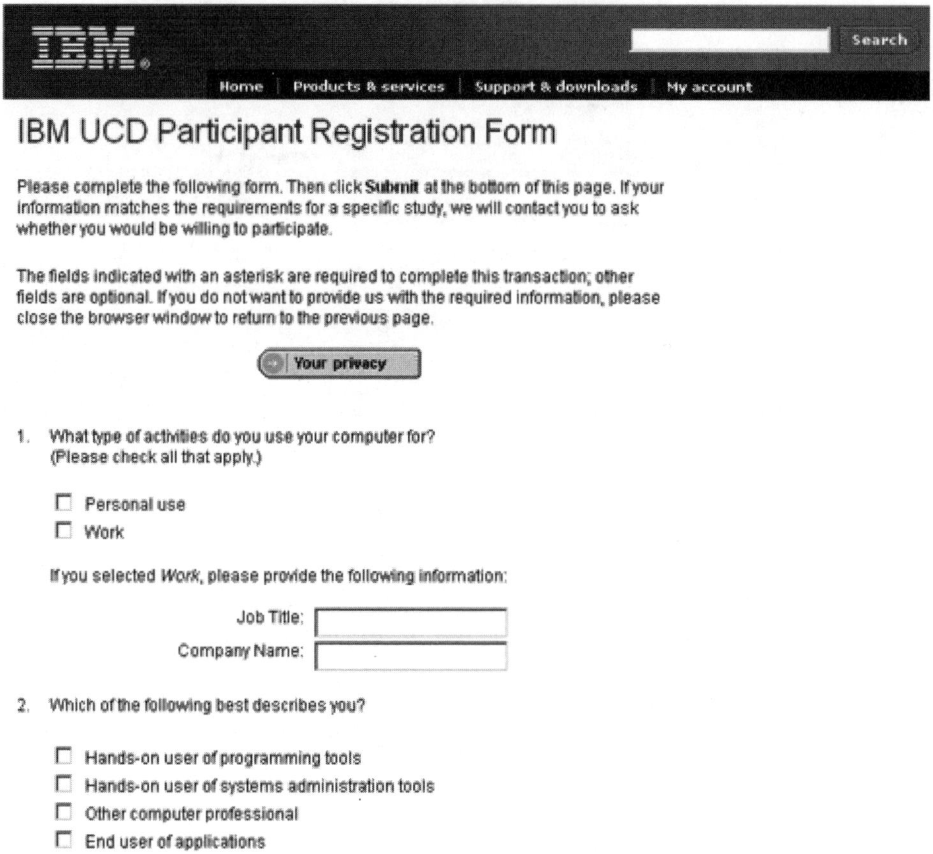

IBM

Search

Home | Products & services | Support & downloads | My account

IBM UCD Participant Registration Form

Please complete the following form. Then click **Submit** at the bottom of this page. If your information matches the requirements for a specific study, we will contact you to ask whether you would be willing to participate.

The fields indicated with an asterisk are required to complete this transaction; other fields are optional. If you do not want to provide us with the required information, please close the browser window to return to the previous page.

Your privacy

1. What type of activities do you use your computer for?
(Please check all that apply.)

- ☐ Personal use
- ☐ Work

If you selected *Work*, please provide the following information:

Job Title:

Company Name:

2. Which of the following best describes you?

- ☐ Hands-on user of programming tools
- ☐ Hands-on user of systems administration tools
- ☐ Other computer professional
- ☐ End user of applications

FIGURE 5.8
IBM participant registration form. (Courtesy of IBM.)

Designers and other practitioners within the company then use the intranet query interface (see Figure 5.9) to the database to select random samples of particular customer characteristics for specific studies, of whatever type. If a Web-based survey will be conducted with the selected sample, the e-mail addresses are used to invite potential participants. The query interface also records the studies for which the names were used to avoid participant study fatigue.

To ensure that the database is as representative of the population of customers as possible, the team should identify the list of market segments,

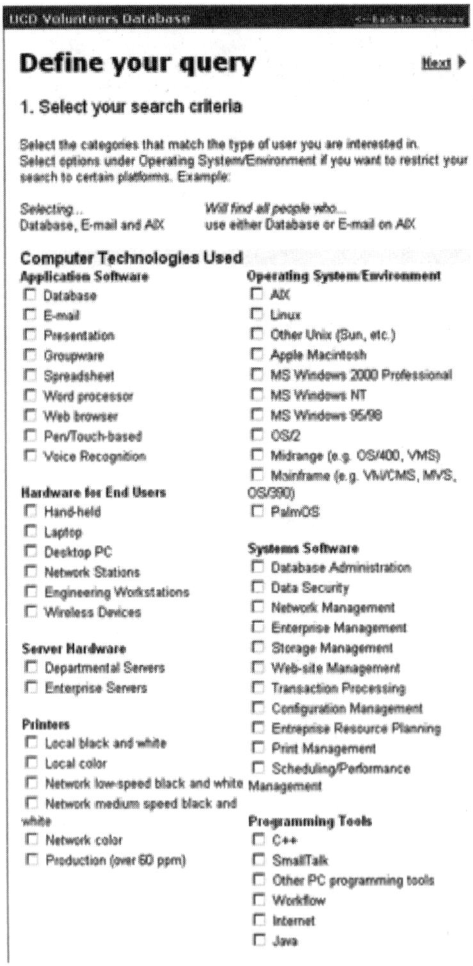

FIGURE 5.9
Recruiting database query interface. (Courtesy of IBM.)

products, and customer types that the company targets with their products. Then, find the usenet groups that the customers in these categories use frequently and invite those visiting the usenet groups to help in the design of products by registering themselves in the database.

To increase the response rate, an incentive should be offered. For example, in the past at IBM, a notebook computer has been offered to a randomly selected respondent. At other times, Amazon.com gift certificates have been used. To address representativeness and to guard against bias in the sample, the team should also regularly check the demographics of people in the database with demographic information available on selected populations. The team has recently also included the company product registration database records into the recruiting database to increase representativeness further. Designers and other practitioners can now identify and invite a sample of representative users *within minutes* of their using this database.

When using technologies like these for UCD, you should ensure that you do not contact the same customer too many times in a specified period of time. Contacting users too often can lead to what is referred to as *study fatigue,* or in the case of surveys *survey fatigue.* The ease and power of using the Internet for interacting with customers has led to a situation where many people experience e-mail overload. The way to avoid unnecessarily contributing to this with your technology-optimized UCD work is to keep track of each of your interactions with your customers and to put in place a guideline regarding how often particular customers may be contacted during a specified period of time. A central recruiting database is an ideal place to implement a policy for this. Access to particular customers' records can be temporarily suspended if the numbers of times the customer has been contacted within a particular period has been exceeded. It is critically important to address this topic when using these technologies for UCD because you do not want to lower your customers' satisfaction by contacting them too often when your overall objective in doing UCD on the project is to increase satisfaction.

Web-Enabled Studies

The Web provides a great opportunity to gather specific information and to conduct user studies very quickly. There are two categories of studies—synchronous and asynchronous. *Synchronous studies* involve conducting studies with one participant at a time in sessions with a UCD facilitator where the user and the facilitator are in different locations. *Asynchronous studies* involve conducting studies with a large number of users with no facilitator present. Both of these types of Web-enabled studies have significant benefits.

- They allow UCD practitioners to get customer input from a worldwide audience. A major problem with most studies done in a UCD lab is that they are typically done with participants selected from the immediate area surrounding the development location. Most hardware and software products are, as a result, designed specifically for North American customers due to this bias. It is possible to have a more representative set of customers participate by either flying in participants or taking portable UCD lab facilities to the participants' locations. Although these alternatives are used to some degree, they are often too prohibitively expensive to do on a regular basis. Web-enabled studies provide a cost-effective way to achieve the benefits of worldwide involvement without the time and expense.

- They provide a mechanism to involve customers who do not feel comfortable or for whom it may be difficult to visit a physical UCD lab facility and who may not want to have UCD practitioners come to visit them at their locations. Customers may include groups such as information technology professionals (programmers, system administrators, database administrators, etc.), executives, homemakers, and individuals with various disabilities. Without the use of these types of tools, many of these customers would not be represented in the samples used for studies. In turn, their input would not be reflected in the design of the product or system.

- They encourage more frequent and rapid gathering of input from customers with sessions of lesser duration than traditional approaches. Teams often need customer input on design issues that arise, and it is critical to get input in a timely way. If a panel of customers who have agreed to be involved in feedback for the project is set up, teams can often get customer input in a matter of hours using these methods.

- They represent a more ecologically valid context to collect information from customers. Bringing customers into a UCD lab involves taking them from their regular environment—their own computer, the usual background noise, and interruptions—and placing them in a new environment. These new tools allow customers to stay in their own environment while giving their input.

Each of the two types of Web-enabled studies will be described in turn.

Synchronous Virtual Testing

Synchronous virtual testing retains many of the advantages of running an individual study with participants in addition to the benefits outlined earlier. The only disadvantages of this method are that it does not allow the level of interpersonal rapport found in face-to-face in-person studies and that facial expressions and other nonverbal feedback are not typically captured. However, the advantages far outweigh the disadvantages of conducting this type of session.

Setting up and conducting synchronous virtual testing sessions involves acquiring software that allows the UCD practitioner's computer (or one in their UCD lab) to be linked to a participant's computer using the Internet. A number of products can be used for this type of testing. Perhaps the most popular is Microsoft Windows NetMeeting. This tool comes with the Windows operating systems starting with 2000 and is available as a free download for earlier versions of Windows. It is easy to set up and use in situations where it does not have to go through an Internet firewall. Consequently, it is a good way to run test sessions for internal applications where UCD practitioners and users are both on a company intranet and behind a company firewall. It is also appropriate for studies run outside companies and with users who are not behind a firewall. However, the majority of situations increasingly involve firewalls. A popular alternative to NetMeeting is IBM's Lotus Sametime (Figure 5.10). Sametime has the added benefit of combining the technology for sharing applications across computers with an instant messaging component that is very useful for communications between the UCD practitioner and the participant at times when a telephone link is not being used. It is also possible to include video of both the practitioner and the customer if both have Internet cameras. However, the effectiveness of these elements depends on the Internet connection speed involved. Other products that can be used to run synchronous virtual user sessions exist, but these are, in our experience, the most effective. Both of these are also easy to use in that separate software typically does not need to be installed. NetMeeting is included in the latest Microsoft operating systems, and Sametime works within a browser.

An actual session involves conducting the test in the same way as would be done if both practitioner and participant were in a UCD lab. The difference is that the participant accesses the application being tested via the Internet. Interaction with the user is done either via a telephone link, an instant messaging session, or both. The usual hardcopy forms and question-

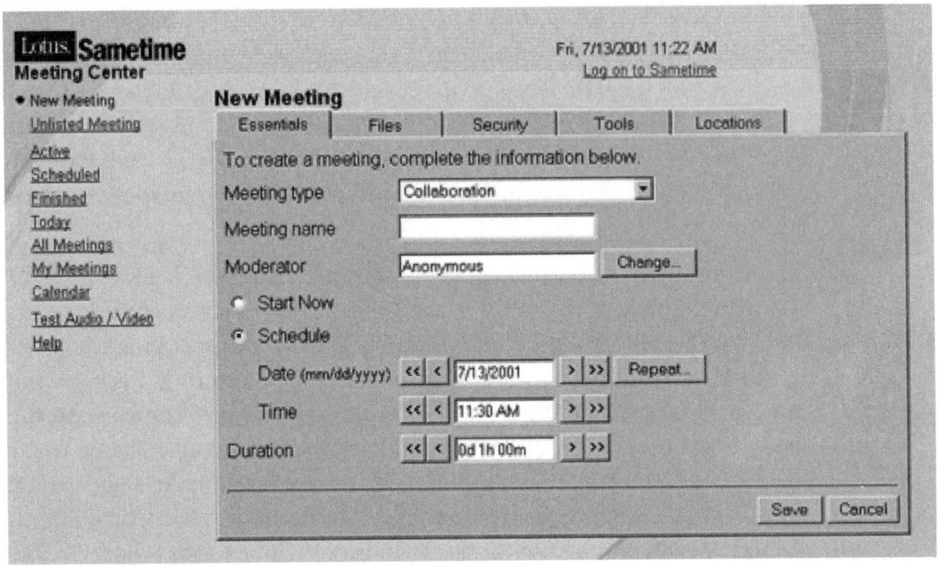

FIGURE 5.10
Lotus Sametime. (Courtesy of IBM.)

naires typically used in a face-to-face session can be delivered via the Web or you can use the tools described in the next section.

Asynchronous Web Surveys

The primary advantage of asynchronous Web surveys is the capability of getting input from a large number of customers very quickly. This feature is particularly useful for validating information collected from small samples of participants in UCD lab settings, for example. It is also critically important to collect certain types of information from customers where small or unrepresentative samples would be entirely inappropriate. This case occurs when collecting information on nonperformance-based issues like preferences. The visual design of products and systems is getting increasingly important. However, conducting a UCD lab study with five users to determine the preferred color and graphical elements of an interface is insufficient. In the case of design issues like this, a large geographically diverse sample is required, and an asynchronous Web survey is the ideal tool to use to collect the feedback.

Web surveys can be constructed in a variety of ways. A survey can be built by "hand coding" an HTML form and writing a script program of some type to collect the data. Although this method allows for the greatest degree of freedom in the design of the survey, it is also the most time consuming and requires the most technical skill. There are a variety of products available that drastically reduce the time and skill required for developing effective surveys. A number of companies develop surveys as a service, but we will here focus on the ways that you can create these surveys in the most cost-effective way with tools.

IBM's Lotus Domino, for example, can be used to develop standard survey templates and have them delivered to UCD practitioners across a company in a survey wizard such as the one shown in Figure 5.11.

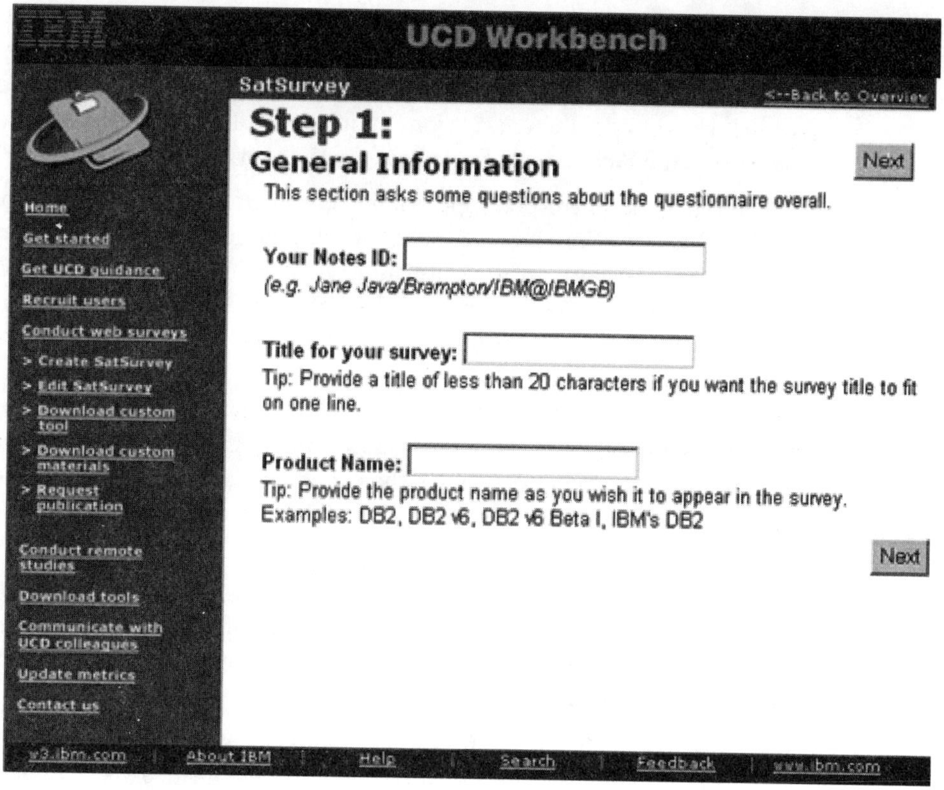

FIGURE 5.11
Survey wizard. (Courtesy of IBM.)

The wizard provides survey templates for conducting the most commonly required surveys, including customer satisfaction, requirements gathering, and user problem determination. The creation of the surveys is automated so that practitioners can simply provide the product name and questions they would like to ask in addition to a standard set and then press OK to put the survey on the Web. Setting up this type of system involves some work initially by a programmer in the company, but, after that, this method is probably the most rapid approach for creating surveys for UCD practitioners to use.

If your company does not have access to the resources to put this type of system in place, UCD practitioners can use one of the available Web authoring tools to construct the survey. These tools include NetObjects Fusion, Microsoft FrontPage, and Macromedia Dreamweaver. The advantage of using these tools is that the overall look and placement of all elements on the survey can be precisely controlled and images, screenshots, and other elements can be easily incorporated. The disadvantage of using these tools is that the practitioner needs to do additional work to collect and analyze the results. However, if there is a strong requirement for exact placement of elements into the Web survey, then these are the tools to consider.

The best general-purpose approach to conducting Web surveys is to use a product like WebSurveyor. It includes wizards for constructing the questions for the survey and for publishing it. WebSurveyor is composed of a desktop component and a server. The latter can be hosted on a company intranet server or on WebSurveyor's servers. The desktop tool includes the ability to define a display file, which is a way of creating a look for the survey visuals to ensure that they are consistent with your own company's branding and Web standards. Although it includes an extensive set of standard response formats, it also has the capability for easily creating and saving customized ones. See Figures 5.12 and 5.13 for examples of WebSurveyor screens.

The disadvantage of a solution like WebSurveyor is that the format of the questions is fixed, and it is difficult to incorporate images like screen captures into the survey. However, it is a very effective and efficient tool for conducting asynchronous Web surveys.

Another form of asynchronous Web survey serves many of the same needs as those described thus far but is more free form. This type of survey involves setting up a discussion forum for a panel of customers on which UCD practitioners can post design issue questions and ask users to submit their input. It can be set up by using products like IBM's Lotus QuickPlace.

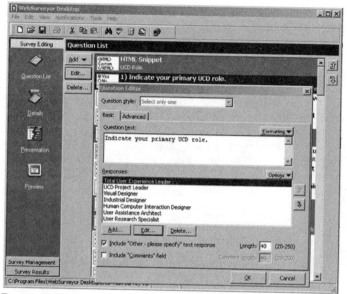

FIGURE 5.12

Constructing a survey with WebSurveyor. (Courtesy of WebSurveyor.)

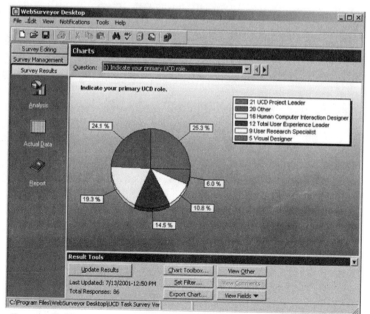

FIGURE 5.13

Analyzing a survey with WebSurveyor. (Courtesy of WebSurveyor.)

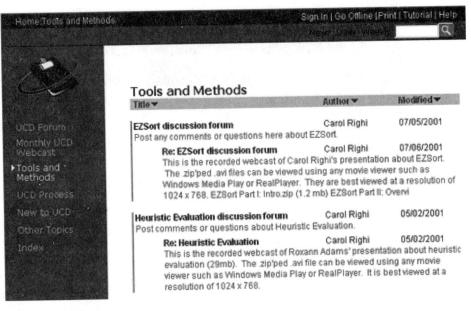

FIGURE 5.14
QuickPlace discussion. (Courtesy of IBM.)

A UCD practitioner can set up a discussion forum with no programming, set permissions for particular users to have access to particular parts of the forum, and include screen capture images, descriptions of design ideas, and forms for providing ratings. Customers providing input can respond to the questions in the forms but can also attach a screen capture image, for example, to illustrate a particular idea. Customers can log onto the QuickPlace to provide their input, but they can also send information via e-mail to the QuickPlace's e-mail address. They can also set a preference asking to have updates to the QuickPlace automatically forwarded to them in an e-mail message. Teams have found QuickPlace a great way to keep the communication with their customers informal, frequent, and bidirectional. See Figure 5.14 for an example of a QuickPlace database.

Other more elaborate and expensive solutions are available in the category of Web-enabled studies. In fact, some attempt to incorporate elements of the synchronous virtual testing into an asynchronous Web survey solution. A solution from Vividence is a good example. This solution is only relevant to Web site design, but it incorporates a number of key elements into a single system together with a built-in panel of customers. Once set up, a study runs without a UCD practitioner involved even though participants do much of what is done in a traditional study—read a scenario, carry out tasks, report problems they experience, and provide ratings of their experience. Companies like Vividence argue that their tools can serve as a replacement for any other kind of practitioner-facilitated study. We share the view of Tamler (2001) and others. They proposed that these tools are not a replacement but rather a supplement to studies that are UCD practitioner facilitated. Web-enabled studies are important to include in any UCD plan of activities.

UCD Lab Tools

A number of different tools can optimize the operation of a UCD lab. Increasingly, UCD labs have a Group Room with LAN-connected computers for collecting information simultaneously from typically 10 to 20 participants at a time. As pointed out in previous chapters, methods like task analysis and design walkthroughs are very effectively carried out with groups. Key to effectively capturing information is the use of appropriate electronic decision support software. Among the best of these is a product from GroupSystems.com. It allows the simultaneous anonymous collection of participant information during electronic brainstorming, the ability to synthesize large quantities of information into logical groupings, and the capability to execute surveys as well. With this type of tool, UCD teams can run electronic focus groups and avoid the typical pitfalls of using traditional focus groups including the disproportionate influence of one or two vocal participants' views on the group's view, the underrepresentation of less vocal members, and, in turn, the biasing of the session's results. The use of this type of tool also makes the UCD practitioner more productive in that results of a session are available in a file at the end of the session with all the electronic discussion captured in the participants' own words and terminology. A screen capture of the GroupSystems.com electronic brainstorming component is shown in Figure 5.15.

The single-participant UCD lab room and the observer area can be optimized as well. Several tools are relevant here. The first is a logger tool for a UCD practitioner to capture key activities happening during the session for later analysis. Many organizations build their own logger programs. Interestingly, UCD practitioners become attached to their favorite logger program much like programmers who become attached to their preferred editor program. A screen capture of a logger tool used widely within IBM is shown in Figure 5.16.

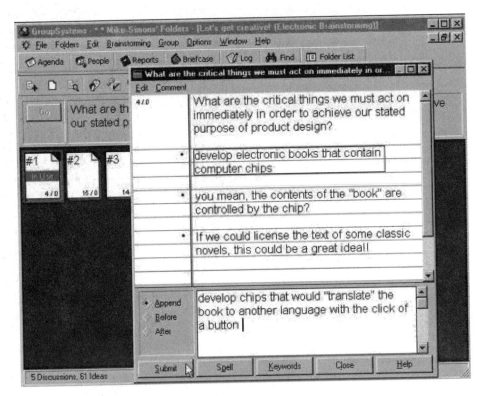

Figure 5.15

Electronic brainstorming. (Courtesy of GroupSystems.com.)

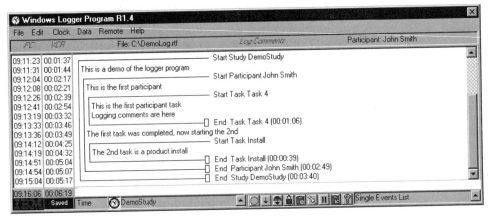

Figure 5.16

Test logger. (Courtesy of IBM.)

This logger tool not only is integrated into a suite of other tools for capturing individual user sessions but also includes a mechanism to capture digital activity on the participant's computer and then to edit it. See Figure 5.17 for a schematic that shows the relationship between these tools. Many organizations still use what is referred to as a "scan converter" to capture images from the participant's computer screen onto videotape in the observation control room. Video editing equipment is then used to select the segments showing particular participants' problems, to put them on a summary tape, and then to show the tape to the other design or development teams and to management. The disadvantages of this approach, however, include the fact that much detail is lost when converting computer screen digital signals to analog video signals. The equipment required to do this type of conversion is typically quite expensive and must be constantly upgraded with each new increase in screen resolution. The LogCam tools used at IBM (Figure 5.17), on the other hand, allow the UCD practitioner to capture user screen activity and to save it at the same fidelity, the editing process can be conducted on a UCD practitioner's own computer, and summary screen segments in .avi format can be easily attached to documents or placed on Web servers allowing anyone on the team to view the files in streaming format on their own browsers.

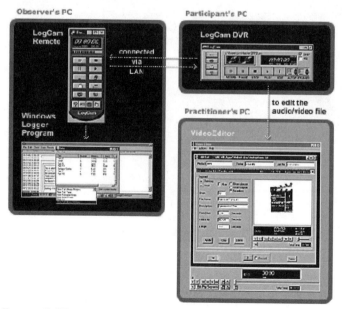

FIGURE 5.17
A set of tools for usability testing. (Courtesy of IBM.)

Automated Usage Capture

As pointed out earlier, much of the information typically collected from users lacks ecological validity in that participants are often not using the product in their natural environment doing their own work. When information is collected in the natural environment, such as during beta testing, insufficient information is typically collected.

Many organizations have built custom tools that instrument the code in an application or tool in various ways. The tools then write all participant activity to a file and practitioners can then see everything the participant did during a session. IBM-specialized tools (Figure 5.18) make it possible to monitor (with a customer's knowledge and consent) key behaviors with a product (i.e., the number of times a customer used a particular part of a product, the number of invocations of a help window, and what windows just preceded it), store context-rich information about particular events (i.e., all screen activity in the four minutes preceding a user-identified significant event such as a problem), and automatically send the information back to the design team. These tools can be run either unattended or with the user signaling key events. All these tools have dramatically increased the ability of UCD practitioners to gather user information rapidly and effectively.

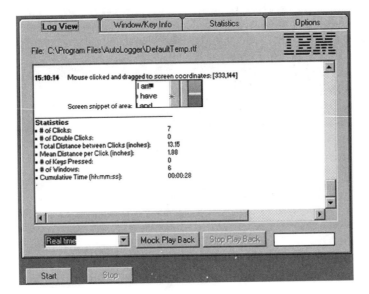

FIGURE 5.18
Automated usage report from an IBM tool. (Courtesy of IBM.)

Information Analysis and Interpretation_____

A key area for which tools are required involves the analysis and interpretation of customer information. A UCD practitioner typically has a great deal of information from customers on a project and very little time in which to analyze and make sense of it. Although the typical statistics software packages can be used for many types of information, there are certain types of information for which a unique solution is required. One such area involves dealing with card sort information. The card sort technique can be very effectively used to gather information from customers on the types of information they would expect to see on a Web site, for example, and then to sort the individual pieces of information into categories that make sense to the customer. The results of such an exercise can provide designers with information about what items should be on the navigator bar, for example. The challenge is dealing with the amount of data this involves and the proper statistical analyses that should be carried out on them to make the information maximally useful and reliable. IBM developed a tool for this called EZSort (Figure 5.19), which automates the various stages of the card sort process. The results can be manipulated easily to determine, for example, what might be the items on a navigator bar given a navigator bar length of five items vs. ten items. This analysis can be accomplished by simply moving a vertical bar on the interface.

Tracking Progress _____

As pointed out in Chapters 2 and 3, a critical ingredient in the effective introduction and deployment of UCD in an organization involves ensuring that project and executive management are aligned. To do so, they must have access to key UCD metrics with which to manage progress. In many organizations, something cannot be managed unless it is measured and tracked. If all other aspects of a product or system have measures in a project status meeting, for example, and UCD attributes do not, then they will get insufficient attention. Therefore, it is important to measure, capture, and track core UCD information.

Case Study: IBM UCD Metrics

- Detailed gathering of key metrics enables IBM to track products' progress.
- Metric summaries provide a tool for highlighting critical aspects of a product's design.

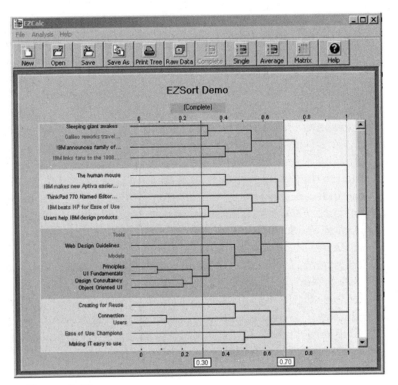

FIGURE 5.19
EZSort for card sort analysis. (Courtesy of IBM.)

- Key metrics include product information, customer feedback,   UCD activities, goals, and specific problem information.

At IBM, UCD Metrics is a core database application that is part of the UCD Workbench used across the company. All UCD projects across all divisions and groups at IBM have their core information in this database. Automated reminder notices are sent once a month, updates are made to each project, and divisional summary reports are automatically generated. The latter are reviewed within each division and by the ease of use champions for each division and the corporate UCD team on a monthly basis. Screen captures of the database, the project form, and the summary report, respectively, are shown in Figures 5.20, 5.21, and 5.22.

The information in the database includes a description of the product (name, version, market segment, release date), the customers, the competition, and the plan information regarding accessibility, ease of use objectives, marketing messages, customer satisfaction, UCD team skills, education, and activity plan, as well as a running capture of user problems and their fix status, the number of user hours

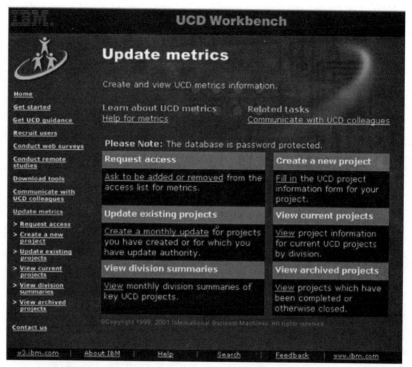

FIGURE 5.20
UCD Metrics database. (Courtesy of IBM.)

involved in UCD studies, and trade press quotes. The division summaries generated from the database take a snapshot of the key ease of use project information. These summaries not only organize the information for executives into a common format but also highlight early warning information such as a severity 1 user problem that has a fix date beyond the planned release date. This information allows executives to make a conscious decision to change the plan or to continue with the current one with the knowledge that they could be reading about the severity 1 user problem in trade press reports after the ship. UCD is a key part of doing business, and tools like the UCD Metrics database provide executives with the information they need to make business decisions based on good information.

At IBM, the UCD Metrics database has been instrumental in providing focus on UCD. A database like this is used at IBM given its size, number of products, and the available resources. Your organization may not need a database like this. In fact, a spreadsheet asking for this type of information may be quite sufficient for the needs of many companies. However, keep in mind that whatever approach is adopted to track progress, it must be easy to complete, effective at tracking key information,

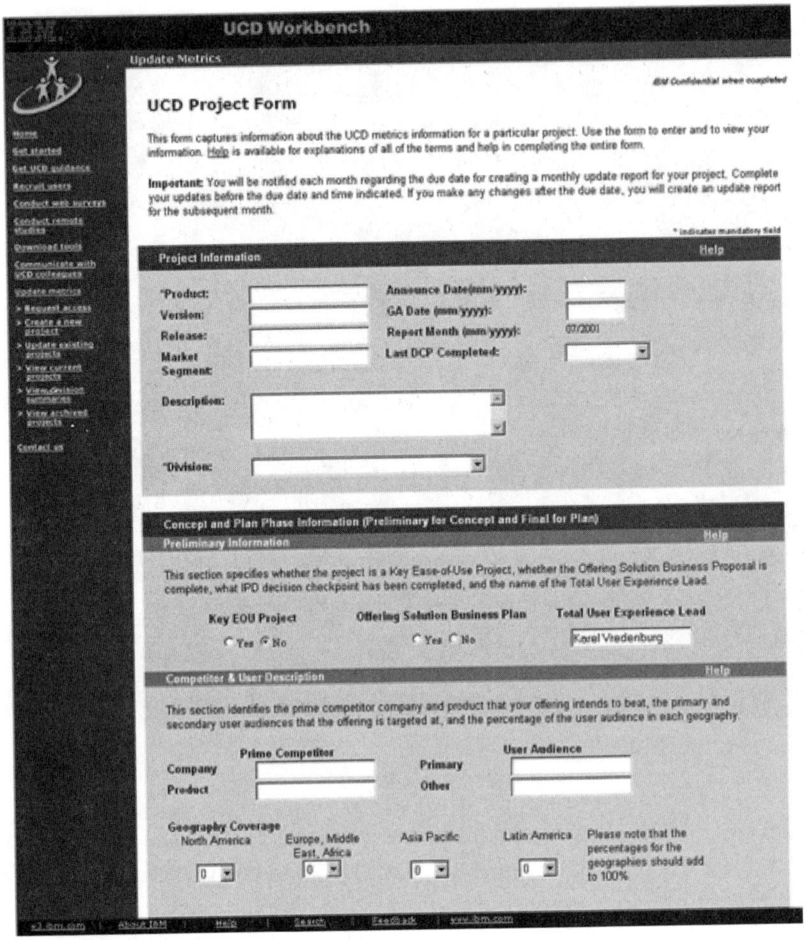

FIGURE 5.21
UCD Metrics project form. (Courtesy of IBM.)

and, most importantly, be part of the management processes at your company. A sample metrics form can be found on the accompanying CD.

Future Trends

The technologies designed with UCD as well as those used to carry out the approach itself have gone through a major transformation over the last few years. At one time, a standard software user interface was a mainframe "green screen" character display, and the associated hardware filled a room.

Category	Subject	A	B
Offering	Product Name		
	Market Segment		
	Product Description		
IPD	Decision Checkpoint Exited		
	Most Recent Report Update		
	Offering Solutions Business Plan		
Competition	Prime Competitor		
	Product or Project Name		
Users	Primary		
	Secondary		
Global Markets	North America		
	Europe, Middle East, Africa		
	Asia Pacific		
	Latin America		
Accessibility	Checkpoint Score		
	Deviation Request		
	Deviation Approved		
Satisfaction	Previous Release		
	Competition		
	Target		
	Design		
	Development		
	Postship		
UCD	Total User Experience Lead		
	Multidisciplinary Team Skills		
	UCD Education		
	Total User Experience Design		
	Cumulative Total User Hours		
User Problems	Percent Fixed to Date		
	Severity 1 Fixes Exceeding GA		
Marketing	Announce Date		
	Ease-of-Use Message(s)		
	Ease-of-Use Press Quotes		
Details	Link to Project Report		

FIGURE 5.22
UCD Metrics report. (Courtesy of IBM.)

However, we have experienced a transition to graphical windowed interfaces that were constructed out of common components to an early Web interface that allowed full degrees of freedom in designs typically graphically rich, and then to a more structured Web interface, through to a personal digital assistant interface and a cell phone display, both of which are character based. On the hardware side, we have moved to ever-smaller form factors and greater and greater mobility and wirelessness. These trends are shown in Figure 5.23.

Not only are these software and hardware trends continuing, but the old interfaces and form factors are also not going away. It isn't the case that each

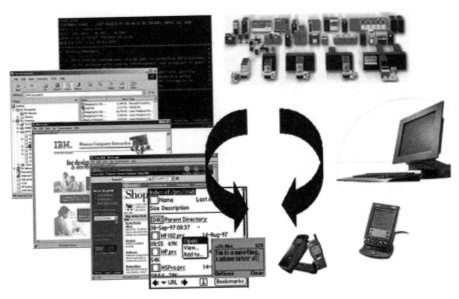

FIGURE 5.23
User interface evolution. (Courtesy of IBM.)

of these advances replaced the previous ones. There are still applications with mainframe interfaces, windowed operating systems still exist despite the introduction of the Web, Web interfaces are still around despite the introduction of PDAs and cell phone interface, and, of course, computers and computing devices of all types and sizes still exist side by side. Today's development teams need to design for all these interfaces and hardware form factors individually. And, even more challenging, they must increasingly design for all of them simultaneously. In other words, a single application may have its data reside on a mainframe computer and have the data accessible from a desktop windows-based application, a Web-based one, and a PDA and/or cell phone. The latter could be accessible via the cell phone display or via a telephony interface.

Add to this challenge the need to design for an ever-widening range of customers. During the time when mainframe computers were the only computers in existence, users were "glass house" technical experts. Compare that with the trends seen today where the Web, PDAs, and cell phones are used by an extremely wide range of customers. "All users" also includes all languages and cultures as well as all levels of ability and disability.

Carrying out UCD appropriately on these projects is even more critical than those for which there were single hardware and software interfaces used by a constrained set of customers. However, it also makes the task of effectively carrying out UCD more difficult. In the future, this difficulty will lead to even greater integration of methods and tools. In fact, it will also involve incorporating these very technologies into the UCD toolset itself.

It is also important to point out that we are also experiencing a trend in customer expectation. In the earliest mainframe-only phases of the computer industry, user expectation was essentially centered around *behavior*—what functions a computer could do that were useful and what was required to get them to be carried out. The second phase involving windowed desktop systems focused on *cognition*—what user actions could be anticipated and done by the computer automatically. The third Web-based phase has had a predominant focus on *affect*—the emotional reactions to highly visual graphical displays. The trend in the future, however, is for *delight*—addressing all these dimensions simultaneously and in all the right amounts. (See Figure 5.24.)

Given the converging hardware and software technology, customer type, and customer expectation trends, what additional enhancements are required to optimize UCD further? The following section will outline the elements that are on the near horizon for UCD.

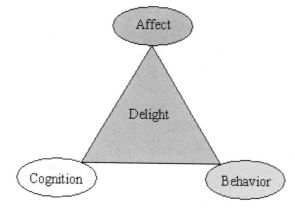

FIGURE 5.24

The evolution toward delight as a customer expectation.

Methodology Integration_____

Chapters 2 and 4 described a series of methods and techniques that are used effectively together to carry out UCD. We have purposely not described these as a *methodology* but rather as an *approach*. We believe that the current set of methodologies that exist, while internally consistent, are insufficient as the only way to do UCD. They are too unidimensional and lack the ability to be able to be applied to a wide range of projects from the very small to the very large. When published, a new methodology is typically illustrated by an example, whether real or fictitious. However, the example is virtually always a simple, straightforward one. The readers of books about these types of methodologies are led to believe, in turn, that the methodologies will work for their own projects. Although some with simple and straightforward projects will be able to apply the methodology, most will not largely due to the fact that their projects are more complex.

Ken Dye of Microsoft discussed the challenge of designing large productivity software suites like Microsoft Office (2001a, 2001b). One of his main arguments is that the current state of knowledge regarding methodologies is likely sufficient for designing specialized applications like banking machines but requires enhancement for designing complex systems such as a general-purpose productivity suite.

The design challenges outlined at the beginning of this section combined with the known limitations of existing methodologies used in isolation particularly with large applications leads to a need to take a more integrated approach to methodologies.

We believe that essentially three core sets of methodologies appear most promising in this regard and are essential to integrate—story-based design, scenario-based design, and model-based design. An illustrated instance of each of these will now be described.

Story-Based Design

The essence of the story-based-design approach is that writing stories is like designing products and that having all the information required to write a good story also leads to good product design (Gruen, 2000). Proponents of story-based design argue that a project should start with an understanding of the typical user of the eventual offering. This understanding is then captured in the development of a persona—a detailed description of a typical user. This description includes the basics such as age and gender, but it also entails an account of their appearance (often with a photograph), work setting (office, cubicle, car, etc.), relationships with coworkers and others, typical activities, likes and dislikes, and preferences. Building on the development of the persona, the team captures a representative task flow into the current story. This story is the *before* instance of the task flow prior to the introduction of what changes the new offering will bring to the situation. Next, the design story is developed illustrating how the typical user's day or series of events would be different given the new offering.

According to proponents of this approach, it is essential to use all that is known about storytelling from industries dealing with books and movies. This corpus includes such things as character development, plot, and dramatic tension. Building in these elements makes stories more realistic, engaging, and compelling. Humans appear to be hardwired to be drawn to the telling of stories and are able to understand information better when presented in this form. So too then when product design is cast in a story format. The design team building the story is better able to ensure that all necessary elements are included, and others are better able to understand a description of the design and its value when presented in a story format. Gruen (2000) points out that if you can't tell a good story about your design, then you likely don't have a good design.

Scenario-Based Design

A wide range of methodologies fall into the scenario-based-design category. However, the essence of scenario-based design (Carroll, 1995; Rosson and Carroll, 2002) is grounding design in an understanding of the interrelation of tasks users carry out over time and the capture and sharing of this information for design. In many ways, whereas story-based design uses elements of fiction writing, scenario-based design uses the techniques of a nonfiction book. Capturing information and conveying it in scenario-based design is more complete and factual. By comparison, story-based design typically only conveys a thin slice through a scenario and builds greater detail and in a dramatic fashion.

The major benefit of scenario-based design is the comprehensive textual descriptions of the context into which designers will be creating a solution.

Model-Based Design

Model-based approaches further increase the level of detail and rigor in specifying the context for design. A well-known version of model-based design is *Object, View, and Interaction Design,* or OVID (Roberts et al., 1998), which was described in Chapter 4. The essence of this approach is making customers experience design more like object-oriented software engineering. The two key elements of software engineering that are the most beneficial are the mathematical rigor involved in specifying the system from a user's perspective and the ease with which the design can be implemented given its specification in software engineering format.

The OVID approach systematically builds various models using standard object-oriented diagramming methods, which start with a specification of the user model. They are iterated on and further detail is built into them. Proponents of model-based approaches stress the degree to which the modeling ensures that all key information issues are addressed in a systematic and rigorous way.

Integration

All three of these methodologies are powerful when used by themselves albeit they all have limitations in certain situations, as pointed out previously. However, there is great value in bringing the advantages of all three into an integrated, new approach.

The story-based approach is best for communicating the design and its value to customers and executives. This format lends itself best to ensuring that the design is correct at the conceptual level. It also reinforces to the design team a picture of actual use that is so simple and compelling that anyone who experiences the story will be able to conjure it up easily from memory at any time during the project. Story-based methods, however, often lack breadth and representativeness. A dramatic story is frequently built at the expense of details and comprehensiveness. Stories in story format are also very difficult for a programming team to implement. Although stories are easy to understand and follow, they lack the format for rigorous specification of elements to program.

The scenario-based approach is more comprehensive and is used to communicate the context for designs to the design team. However, scenarios are less powerful than stories for communicating to customers and executives. Although they typically include more detail, scenarios are often also difficult for programmers to implement.

The model-based approaches are excellent for communicating designs for implementation by programmers and are typically quite complete and comprehensive. However, their major limitation involves communicating the design to customers, executives, and members of the design team who do not have appropriate education and training.

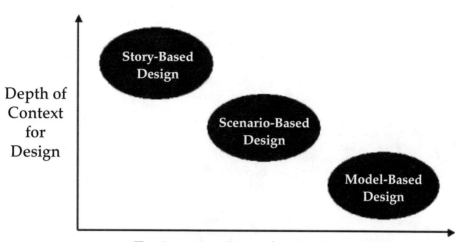

FIGURE 5.25
Comparison of methodologies.

These relative advantages are illustrated in Figure 5.25, contrasting the methodologies along the depth-of-context-for-design and engineering-rigor-for-implementation axes.

The current limitations of each of these methodologies lead to their sub-optimal adoption. An appropriate integration of them will result in the combined benefits of all three and the elimination of their limitations.

Work is currently progressing at IBM on integrating these methodologies (Vredenburg, 2001). A key component is building a central database together with associated tools for the capture of all information. Early work suggests that using such a database and tools will lead to increased *speed* of carrying out UCD, *simplicity* of understanding customer and design information by all constituents (customers, executives, design team, and implementation programmers), and *scalability* for designing systems from the smallest to the largest. The integrated approach will also address the challenges described at the beginning of this section and will be key for the design of projects and systems within the next five years.

The individual tools described throughout this chapter will be linked to and integrated with this core database as depicted in Figure 5.26. Customer information will come into the database via a variety of observation tools, the information and the design based on it will be continually evaluated by

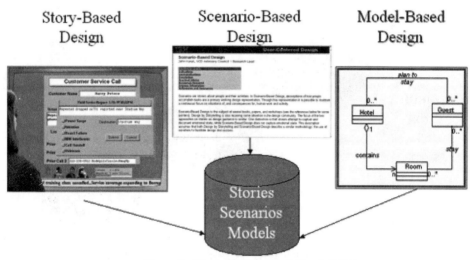

FIGURE 5.26
Integration of methodologies. (Courtesy of IBM.)

users, and current usage information will be automatically captured and loaded into the database.

Information in the database will, in turn, be able to be shown in a variety of views depending on the type of user of the information. Customers may be able to see a story view; programmers, a model view; and executives, a view customized for them.

The integrated UCD approach described in this book is today's state-of-the-art, proven way to develop a compelling total customer experience for products and systems. The tools described in this chapter provide practitioners with ways to further optimize today's UCD methods. This section outlined how UCD will be further integrated and optimized in the future both in terms of methodologies and technologies.

Keeping Abreast of Improvements

The field of UCD is fast-moving. New techniques, technologies, and methodologies are introduced all the time. There are several ways to keep up with these changes and, in fact, to help direct them and even possibly to create them. To do so, it is important to participate in one or more of the professional organizations that exist in the field and to participate in their conferences and visit their Web sites regularly. The most relevant organizations are outlined here, and their Web site address links are included in the accompanying CD.

- **Usability Professionals' Association (UPA).** For people new to the field of UCD, the UPA is the most appropriate to join first. Although UPA has increased its focus on issues of concern to experts in the field, it is still the organization that has the most information for those new to the field. It is also the organization that has the highest proportion of practitioners, as opposed to scientists and researchers. Its focus is mostly on software and the Web. UPA runs an annual conference, typically in the early summer.

- **ACM Computer-Human Interaction (CHI).** The Association for Computer Machinery special interest group on Computer-Human Interaction is by far the largest association of professionals in the field. It caters to medium-level to expert-level professionals and includes a good proportion of academic researchers. Although it focuses on hardware and software, its primary emphasis is on software and the Web. Recently, CHI is emphasizing a Practitioners' track, as well as its traditional tracks. CHI runs an annual conference, usually in the spring.

- **Human Factors and Ergonomics Society (HFES).** HFES predates the previous two and focuses on hardware as well as software. It deals with a very large range of topics going far beyond the computer industry. Topics include pilot error rate differences with alternative arrangements of instruments on a flight deck instrument display. HFES holds an annual conference, typically in the fall.

In addition to these associations of professionals in the field, there are also many excellent Web sites and publications. Our recommendations regarding the best of these are included on the accompanying CD.

Appendices

We have included material on the accompanying CD that you will be able to use in your introduction, deployment, and/or optimization UCD in your organization Some of this material is also presented here in the appendices. Appendix A shows the slides of the sample presentation "Overview of User-Centered Design" which can be used to introduce an organization to UCD. Appendix B shows an example of a UCD plan template that can be used to capture project status on a monthly basis and reviewed by executives.

Appendix A

User-Centered
Design

IBM.

UCD Overview

© Copyright, International Business Machines,
1997, 1998, 2000, 2001   All Rights Reserved

make **IT** easy

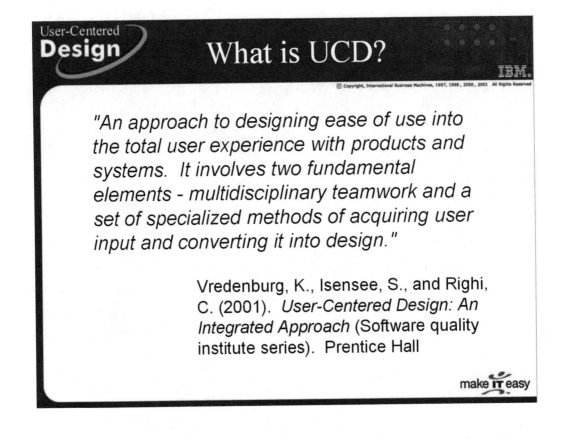

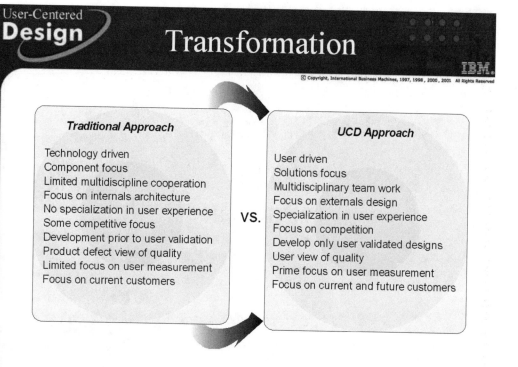

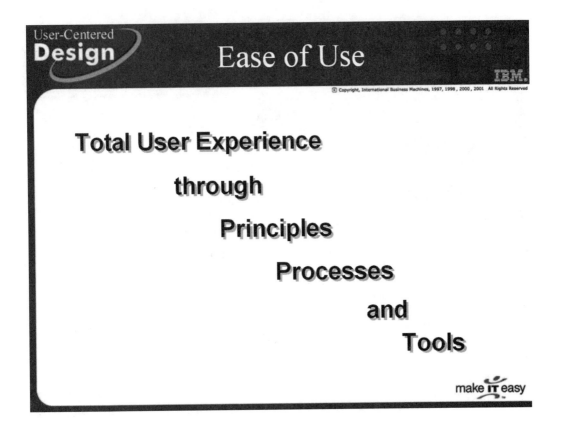

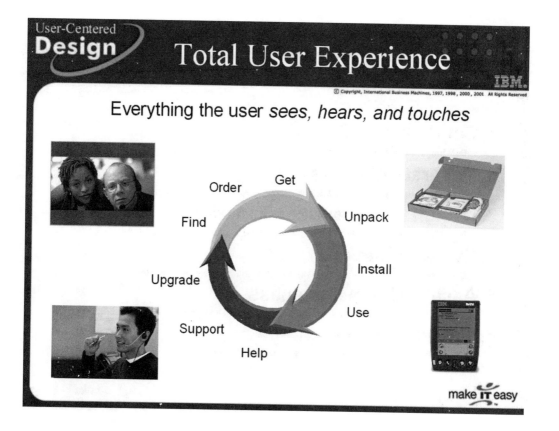

UCD Principles

User-Centered Design

IBM.

1. Set Business Goals
Determining the market, users, and competition to target is central

2. Understand Users
An understanding of the users is the driving force behind all design.

3. Design the Total User Experience
Everything a user sees and touches is designed together by a multidisciplinary team

4. Evaluate Designs
User feedback is gathered often and drives product design and development.

5. Assess Competitiveness
Competitive design requires a relentless focus on the competition and its customers.

6. Manage for Users
User Feedback is integral to product plans, priorities, and decision making.

make IT easy

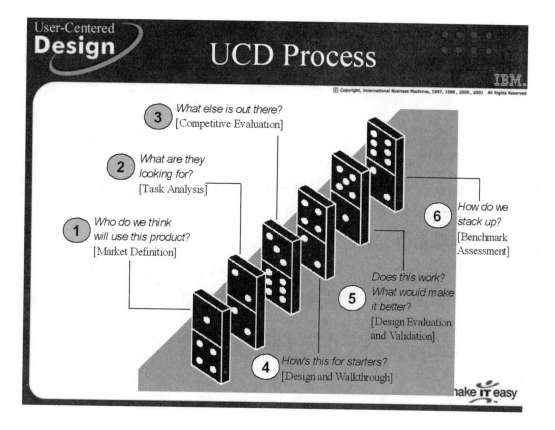

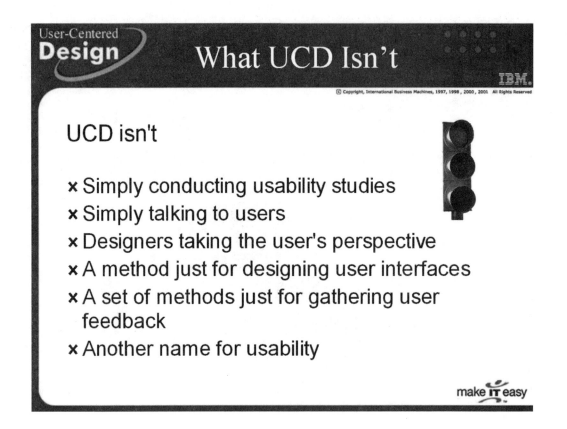

What UCD Isn't

UCD isn't

- × Simply conducting usability studies
- × Simply talking to users
- × Designers taking the user's perspective
- × A method just for designing user interfaces
- × A set of methods just for gathering user feedback
- × Another name for usability

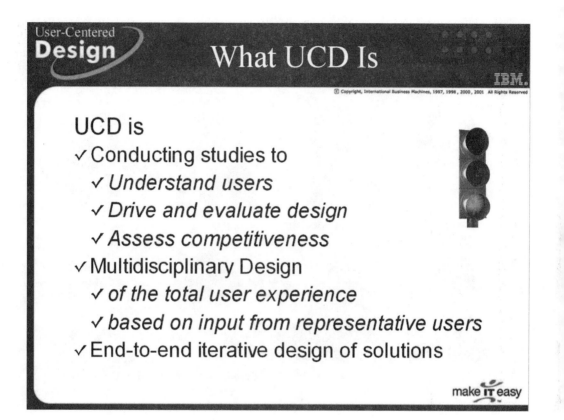

User-Centered Design

The UCD Team

IBM.

© Copyright, International Business Machines, 1997, 1998, 2000, 2001   All Rights Reserved

Total User Experience Leader   Marketing Specialist   Visual Designer   HCI Designer

User Research Specialist   Technology Architect   Service & Support Specialist   User Assitance Architect

make IT easy

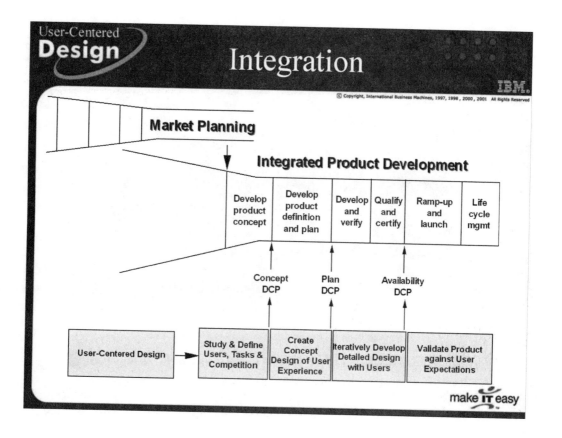

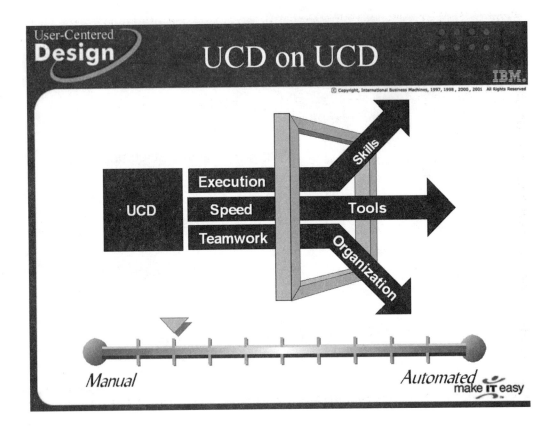

Skills

User-Centered **Design**

IBM.

To get IBM teams enabled and optimized for UCD, we run...

Executive Workshops
  Half-day case-based session
  Senior and middle management
Introduction to UCD Classes
  One-day awareness and overview
  Entire product team
UCD Practitioner Workshops
  Two-day hands-on experience building
  Project UCD Team
Monthly Technical Vitality Webcasts
Yearly Conferences

make **IT** easy

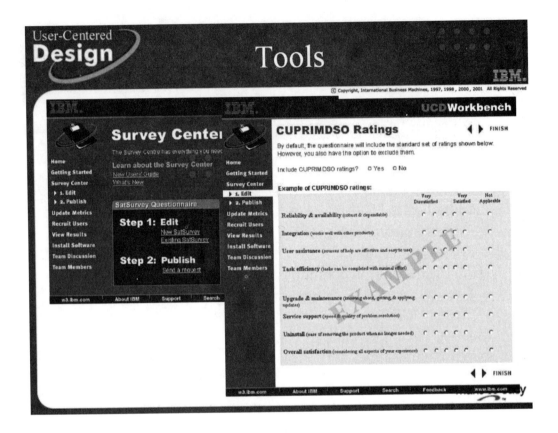

User-Centered **Design**

Tools

IBM®

File Edit View Favorites Tools Help   Links »

IBM®
Home | News | Products | Services | Solutions | About IBM   ShopIBM Support Download

Product XYZ Survey

About your privacy...IBM respects your privacy. The i
the purpose of this study; it will not be used to contact
such purpose. For more information about IBM's policie

Please rate your *satisfaction* with XY

Satisfaction with XYZ Overall

Overall Satisfaction
Considering all aspects of your experience, how w
rate your level of satisfaction?
Capability
How satisfied are you that it has the necessary fun
and features to perform as expected?
Usability
How satisfied are you with the 'ease of use'?
Performance
How satisfied are you with the response time or sp
which it executes its functions?
Reliability
How satisfied are you with 'reliability', that is the
frequency, number, and seriousness of errors.
Installability

Netscape
File Edit View Go Communicator Help

ScoreCard

Attribute	#	Average Rating	% Satisfied		% Satisfied
Overall Satisfaction	57	3.2	37		
Capability	56	3.2	41		
Usability	57	2.8	35		
Performance	56	2.9	34		
Reliability	56	3.5	54		
Installability	44	2.8	32		
Maintainability	35	2.8	29		
Information	52	3.1	33		
Service Support	47	3.7	64		

Document Done

make **IT** easy

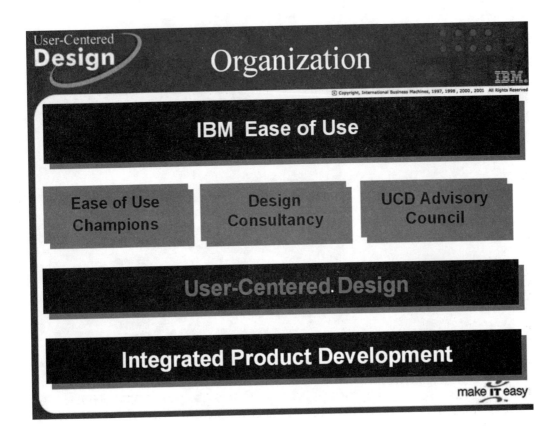

Appendix B

UCD Project Plan and Status

Offering information	
Product name	\<name of product>
Version/Release number	\<version or release number>
Product Description	\<high-level description of product>
Announce date	\<date product will be announced as available>
Market segment(s)	\<describe key market segments. Include percentages, if available>
Concept/Plan phase information	
Key project?	\<indicate if this project has been targeted as a key strategic project>
Business plan?	\<business plan in place? if yes, give reference>
Total User Experience lead	\<team member responsible for overall TUE design>
Competition	
Prime Competitor (company)	\<indicate company that makes prime competitor product>
Prime Competitor (product)	\<indicate product holding desired market share>
User audience (primary)	\<describe primary audience for that product>
User audience (others)	\<describe other audiences for that product>
Geography	\<list geographies in which product is available.
Accessibility Plan	
Attached checklists	\<attach applicable accessibility checklists>
Deviation required?	\<rationale and approvals>
Ease-of-use Objectives	\<repeat next three lines for as many objectives as required>
• Objective	\<state the ease-of-use objective in measurable terms>
• Validation method	\<indicate how this will be assess, i.e., which UCD method>
• Status	\<indicate status of achievement>
Ease-of-use marketing messages	\<indicate marketing tag lines, etc.>
User Satisfaction	
Previous	\<satisfaction ratings for previous version>
Competition	\<satisfaction ratings for competitor>
Target	\<target satisfaction rating>

UCD Team	
UCD Team in place:	
Marketing	<yes or no, plans>
Development	<yes or no, plans>
Visual/Industrial Design	<yes or no, plans>
HCI Design	<yes or no, plans>
User Assistance	<yes or no, plans>
User Research	<yes or no, plans>

UCD Activity Plan	
Audience definition	<indicate date for completing this activity>
Understand User and Competition	<indicate date for completing this activity>
Total User Experience design	<indicate date for completing this activity>
Refine and Evaluate Design	<indicate date for completing this activity>
Assess Postship Satisfaction	<indicate date for completing this activity>

Education	
Leadership workshop	<status, plans>
Introduction	<status, plans>
Team Workshop	<status, plans>
Other	<status, plans>

User Problem Summary	Number	Fixed	Target
Severity 1	<n of problems>	<percent fixed>	<target fix rate>
Severity 2	<n of problems>	<percent fixed>	<target fix rate>
Severity 3	<n of problems>	<percent fixed>	<target fix rate>

User Hours	In-person	Remote	Total
Understand	<n hours>	<n hours>	<n hours>
Evaluate	<n hours>	<n hours>	<n hours>
Test	<n hours>	<n hours>	<n hours>

Life Cycle Phase Information	
Customer satisfaction	<actual satisfaction rating>

Bibliography

P. Adler and Terry Winograd 1992. *USABILITY: Turning Technologies into Tools.* Oxford University Press.

Penny Bauersfeld 1994. *Software by Design: Creating People Friendly Software.* M&T Books.

Hugh Beyer and Karen Holtzblatt 1997. *Contextual Design: A Customer-Centered Approach to Systems Designs.* Morgan Kaufman.

Randolph Bias and Deborah Mayhew 1994. *Cost-Justifying Usability.* Academic Press.

B. Boar 1984. *Application Prototyping: A Requirements Definition Strategy for the 80s.* John Wiley & Sons.

Grady Booch 1994. *Object-Oriented Analysis and Design.* Benjamin/Cummings.

Frederick P. Brooks, Jr. 1982. *The Mythical Man-Month: Essays on Software Engineering.* Addison-Wesley.

John M. Carroll (ed.) 1995. *Scenario-Based Design: Envisioning Work and Technology in Systems Development.* John Wiley & Sons.

Steven Casey 1993. *Set Phasers on Stun.* Aegean Publishing Company.

227

B. Catterall, B. Taylor, and M. Galer 1991. The HUFIT planning, analysis, and specification toolset: Human factors and a normal part of the IT product design process. In *Taking Software Seriously*, ed. J. Karat. Academic Press.

Jacob Cohen 1988. *Statistical Power Analysis for the Behavioral Sciences*, 2d ed. Academic Press.

Dave Collins 1995. *Designing Object-Oriented User Interfaces*. Benjamin/Cummings Publishing.

Alan Cooper 1995. *About Face: The Essentials of User Interface Design*. IDG Books.

E. Del Gado and Jakob Nielsen (eds.) 1996. *International User Interfaces*. John Wiley & Sons.

J. Dumas and Janice Redish 1993. *A Practical Guide to Usability Testing*. Ablex.

K. Dye 2001a. Why is software poorly designed. *Make IT Easy Conference*. June 2001.

K. Dye 2001b. As easy to use as a banking machine. *British Human-Computer Interaction Conference*. 2001.

K. Ericsson and H. Simon 1985. *Protocol Analysis: Verbal Reports as Data*. MIT Press.

Susan Fowler 1998. *GUI Design Handbook*. McGraw-Hill.

Susan Fowler and V. Stanwick 1995. *The GUI Style Guide*. AP Professional.

W. Galitz 1997. *The Essential Guide to User Interface Design*. Wiley.

W. Galitz 1993. *User Interface Screen Design*. QED.

D. Gruen 2000. Beyond scenarios: The role of storytelling in CSCW design. *Computer Supported Cooperative Work Conference*.

Joanne Hackos and Janice Redish 1998. *User and Task Analysis for Interface Design*. John Wiley & Sons.

Paul Heckel 1991. *The Elements of Friendly Software Design*. Sybex.

Martin Helander, Thomas Landauer, and P. Prabhu (eds.) 1997. *Handbook of Human-Computer Interaction*, second edition. North-Holland.

Deborah Hix and H. Rex Hartson 1993. *Developing User Interfaces: Ensuring Usability Through Product and Process*. Wiley Professional Computing.

IBM 1999. *Mastering the Obvious: Why Ease of Use Is Critical to E-Business Success*. IBM.

IBM 1992. *Object-Oriented Interface Design: IBM Common User Access Guidelines*. Que.

International Standards Organization 1989. *Human-Centered Design Processes for Interactive Systems*. International Standards Organization.

Scott Isensee, Ken Kalinoski, and Karl Vochatzer 2000. Designing Internet appliances at Netpliance. In *Information Appliances and Beyond*. Morgan Kaufmann Publishers.

Scott Isensee and James Rudd 1996. *The Art of Rapid Prototyping: User Interface Design for Windows and OS/2*. International Thompson Computer Press.

Scott Isensee and Karel Vredenburg 2000. User-Centered Design and development. In *Constructing Superior Software*. Macmillan Technical Publishing.

Ivar Jacobson 1992. *Object-Oriented Software Engineering: A Use Case Driven Approach*. Addison-Wesley.

P.W. Jordan 2000. *Designing Pleasurable Products: An Introduction to the New Human Factors*. Taylor-Francis.

Thomas K. Landauer 1996. *The Trouble with Computers: Usefulness, Usability, and Productivity*. MIT Press.

Gitte Lindgaard 1994. *Usability Testing and System Evaluation: A Guide for Designing Useful Computer Systems*. Chapman and Hall.

Theo Mandel 1997. *The Elements of User Interface Design*. John Wiley & Sons.

Ji-Yi Mao, Karel Vredenburg, Paul W. Smith, and Tom Carey 2001. *User-Centered Design Methods in Practice: A Survey of the State of the Art*. Center for Advanced Studies Conference.

Deborah Mayhew 1992. *Principles and Guidelines in Software User Interface Design*. Prentice-Hall.

Jakob Nielsen 1993. *Usability Engineering*. AP Professional.

Jakob Nielsen (ed.) 1990. *Designing Interfaces for International Use*. Elsevier.

Jakob Nielsen and Robert Mack (eds.) 1994. *Usability Inspection Methods*. John Wiley and Sons.

Jakob Nielsen and R. Molich 1990. Heuristic evaluation of user interfaces. In *Proceedings of CHI Conference on Human Factors in Computing Systems*. ACM, 249–256.

Donald Norman 1990. *The Design of Everyday Things*. Doubleday.

Donald Norman and Stephen Draper 1986. *User-Centered Systems Design: New Perspectives on Human-Computer Interaction*. Lawrence Erlbaum.

Jenny Preece, Yvonne Rogers, Helen Sharp, David Benyon, Simon Holland, and Tom Carey 1994. *Human-Computer Interaction*. Addison-Wesley.

David Redmond-Pyle and Alan Moore 1995. *Graphical User Interface Design and Evaluation: A Practical Process*. Prentice Hall.

Carol Righi 2001. Building the conceptual model and metaphor: The "3x3." In *Design for People by People: Essays on Usability*, ed. R. Branaghan. Usability Professionals' Association, 213–219.

Dave Roberts, Richard Berry, Scott Isensee, and John Mullaly 1998. *Designing for the User with OVID: Bridging User Interface Design and Software Engineering*. Macmillan Technical Publishing.

Mary Beth Rosson and John M. Carroll 2002. *Usability Engineering: Scenario-Based Development of Human-Computer Interaction*. Morgan Kaufmann.

William B. Rouse 1991. *Design for Success: A Human-Centered Approach to Designing Successful Products and Systems*. Wiley Series in Systems Engineering.

Jeffrey Rubin 1994. *Handbook of Usability Testing: How to Plan, Design, and Conduct Effective Tests*. John Wiley & Sons.

Kenneth S. Rubin and Adele Goldberg 1992. *Object Behavior Analysis: Comments of the ACM*, 35:9 (September), 48–62.

James Rumbaugh 1991. *Object-Oriented Modeling and Design*. Prentice-Hall.

Ben Schneiderman 1998. *Designing the User Interface: Strategies for Effective Human-Computer Interaction*. Addison-Wesley.

Ben Schneiderman 1980. *Software Psychology: Human Factors in Computer and Information Systems*. Winthrop.

A. Shepard 1989. Analysis and training in information tasks. In *Task Analysis for Human-Computer Interaction*, ed. D. Diaper. Ellis Horwood.

K. Snyder 1991. *A Guide to Software Usability*. IBM.

Donald Steward 1987. *Software Engineering*. Brooks/Cole.

H.M. Tamler 2001. High-tech versus high-touch: The limits of automation in diagnostic usability testing. *Make IT Easy Conference*, June 2001.

Bruce Tognazzini 1992. *Tog on Interface*. Addison-Wesley.

Karel Vredenburg 2001. IBM: Designing the Total User Experience. *ACM Interactions*, Volume 8.2.

Karel Vredenburg 1999. Increasing Ease of Use: Emphasizing Organizational Transformation, Process Integration, and Method Optimization. *Comments of the ACM*. 42, 67–71.

Karel Vredenburg, Scott Isensee, and Paul McInerney 1998. Getting rapid and representative user input using the web. *Internetworking*, 1:2.

Susan Weinschenk, Pamela Jamar, and Sarah Yeo 1997. *GUI Design Essentials*. John Wiley & Sons.

James Whiteside, John Bennett, and Karen Holtzblatt 1988. Usability Engineering: Our experience and evolution. In *Handbook of Human-Computer Interaction*, ed. M. Helander. North-Holland.

Michael Wiklund 1994. *Usability in Practice: How Companies Develop User-Friendly Products*. AP Professional.

Rebecca Wirfs-Brock, B. Wilkerson, and L. Wiener 1990. *Designing Object-Oriented Software*. Prentice-Hall.

Larry Wood (ed.) 1998. *User Interface Design: Bridging the Gap from User Requirements to Design*. CRC Press.

Carl Zetie 1995. *Practical User Interface Design*. McGraw Hill.

Index

About the Authors

Karel Vredenburg is the Architect and Corporate Champion for User-Centered Design at IBM. He has responsibility for the development of IBM's UCD approaches, methods, and tools, the deployment of them company-wide, and the leadership of IBM's team of UCD practitioners.

Karel joined IBM in 1988 after having done graduate studies, research, and teaching at the University of Toronto. He developed the integrated version of UCD presented in this book at IBM in 1993 and assumed his present company-wide leadership role in 1995. He is a member of IBM's Design Consultancy for Ease of Use, the Ease of Use Progress Management Council, and chairs the UCD Advisory Council.

Karel has written over 75 conference and journal publications. His recent articles include, "Design Brief: Designing the Total User Experience at IBM" which appeared in *ACM Interactions*, and "Increasing Ease of Use: Emphasizing Organizational Transformation, Process Integration, and Method Optimization" which appeared in *Communication of the ACM*. He is a co-author of the book *Constructing Superior Software* available from Macmillan Technical Publishing and is special issue editor of the International Journal of Human-Computer Interaction. Karel is a regular speaker at professional conferences and is frequently invited to speak to major companies about UCD.

Karel is a member of the International Standards Organization (ISO) committee that develops standards such as the *Human-Centred Design of Interactive Systems* (#13407), the National Institute for Standards and Technology (NIST) working group developing a Common Industry Format for Usability Test Reports, and serves on the National Research Council education committee with responsibility for the development of chaired faculty positions for User-Centered Design.

Karel, Scott, and Carol run a workshop series together based on the material in this book entitled "Practical UCD: How to Introduce, Deploy, and Optimize User-Centered Design". The workshop is typically offered at the annual conference of the three major professional organizations: ACM Computer-Human Interaction (CHI), Usability Professionals' Association (UPA), and Human Factors and Ergonomic Society. Introductory, advanced, and executive education as well as consulting services are also available on the material in this book through IBM (visit the "services" section of www.ibm.com/easy).

Karel has written over 75 conference and journal publications. His recent articles include, "Design Brief: Designing the Total User Experience at IBM" which appeared in ACM Interactions, and "Increasing Ease of Use: Emphasizing Organizational Transformation, Process Integration, and Method Optimization" which appeared in Communication of the ACM. He is a co-author of the book Constructing Superior Software available from Macmillan Technical Publishing and is special issue editor of the International Journal of Human-Computer Interaction. Karel is a regular speaker at professional conferences and is frequently invited to speak to major companies about UCD.

Scott Isensee is a user interface architect with BMC Software in Austin, Texas, where he works on user interface design, architecture, guidelines, and methodologies. He previously worked for Netpliance, designing the I-opener information appliance and for IBM where he was team lead of the corporate user interface architecture group, a consultant, and designer of numerous software and hardware products. Scott was lead for a cross-company team (IBM, SUN, HP, and Novell) that defined the UI architecture for the Common Desktop Environment—the GUI used by most UNIX implementations today.

He has served on ISO, ANSI, and W3C committees, writing software user interface and usability standards. He contributed to the CUA, Motif, and CDE style guides. Scott holds 42 U.S. patents for a wide variety of inventions on the Internet, 3-D graphics, user interface controls, and input devices.

Scott holds masters degrees in industrial psychology and computer science. He is a Certified Professional Ergonomist. He is an author of the books *Designing for the User with OVID, The Art of Rapid Prototyping, Information Appliances and Beyond,* and *Constructing Superior Software.*

Scott was the founding editor of *Internetworking,* the online journal of the Internet technical Group. He is a frequent speaker at industry conferences and has published over 100 technical articles.

Carol Righi is president of Righi Interface Engineering, Inc. She has worked in the area of human-computer interaction since 1984, and currently specializes in interaction design. Dr. Righi has designed user interfaces for the World Wide Web, and for desktop, kiosk, and mainframe applications. She has planned and conducted extensive data-gathering activities, including task analysis, heuristic evaluation, competitive evaluation, low-fidelity prototype evaluation, surveys, and traditional usability tests. She has served as manager for numerous design and evaluation efforts. She has developed many educational offerings, including courses in software design and design process, and trained hundreds of students, including numerous multidisciplinary design teams. Dr. Righi has written extensively in the area of human-computer interaction, usability, and UCD, and has presented at numerous professional meetings worldwide.

About the CD

Contents

A CD-ROM accompanying User-Centered Design: An Integrated Approach by Karel Vredenburg, Scott Isensee, and Carol Righi. ISBN: 0-13-091295-6.

The CD for this text contains a file called index.htm, which lists and allows you to access all of the contents of the CD. The index.htm file can be viewed with an appropriate Web browser.

The contents of this CD include the following:

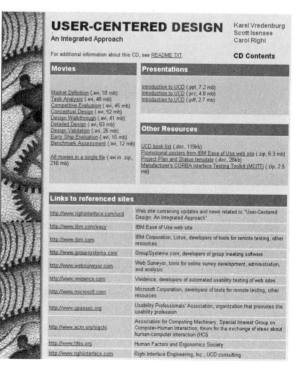

- Movies
  - Market Definition (.avi, 18 mb)
  - Task Analysis (.avi, 48 mb)
  - Competitive Evaluation (.avi, 45 mb)
  - Conceptual Design (.avi, 52 mb)
  - Design Walkthrough (.avi, 41 mb)
  - Detailed Design (.avi, 63 mb)
  - Design Validation (.avi, 26 mb)
  - Early Ship Evaluation (.avi, 15 mb)
  - Benchmark Assessment (.avi, 12 mb)
  - All movies in a single file (.avi in .zip, 216 mb)
- Presentations
  - Introduction to UCD (.ppt, 7.2 mb)
  - Introduction to UCD (.prz, 4.8 mb)
  - Introduction to UCD (.pdf, 2.7 mb)
- Other Resources
  - UCD book list (.doc, 119kb)
  - Promotional posters from IBM Ease of Use web site (.zip, 6.3 mb)
  - Project Plan and Status template (.doc, 28kb)
  - Manufacturer's CORBA Interface Testing Toolkit (MCITT) (.zip, 2.5 mb)
- Links to Sites Referenced in the Book

http://www.righiinterface.com/ucd

Web site containing updates and news related to "User-Centered Design: An Integrated Approach"

http://www.ibm.com/easy

IBM Ease of Use web site

http://www.ibm.com

IBM Corporation, Lotus, developers of tools for remote testing, other resources

http://www.groupsystems.com

GroupSystems.com, developers of group meeting software

http://www.websurveyor.com

Web Surveyor, tools for online survey development, administration, and analysis *http://www.vividence.com*

Vividence, developers of automated usability testing of web sites

http://www.microsoft.com

Microsoft Corporation, developers of tools for remote testing, other resources

http://www.upassoc.org

Usability Professionals' Association, organization that promotes the usability profession

http://www.acm.org/sigchi

Association for Computing Machinery, Special Interest Group on Computer-Human Interaction; forum for the exchange of ideas about human-computer interaction (HCI)

http://www.hfes.org

Human Factors and Ergonomics Society

http://www.righiinterface.com

Righi Interface Engineering, Inc., UCD consulting

System Requirements

- MS Windows 98 or 2000
- At least 800×600 resolution or higher set to 256 colors or more
- Sound card

Software Requirements

To view of the movies:

- Windows Media Player (www.microsoft.com)

Note: For best performance, you should first copy the movie to your hard-drive to view it. To do so, right-click on the Download Now button and select "Save Target As..." (Internet Explorer) or "Save Link As..." (Netscape).

To decompress the .zip files

- WinZip (www.winzip.com)

To see the presentations

- Microsoft PowerPoint (www.microsoft.com)

or

IBM Lotus Freelance Graphics (*www.ibm.com*)

or

Adobe Acrobat Reader (*www.adobe.com*)

- To Read the .doc Files
  Microsoft Word (*www.microsoft.com*)
- To Access the .html Files or Web Sites
  Microsoft Internet Explorer or Netscape Navigator/Communicator

License Agreement

Use of the software accompanying *User-Centered Design: An Integrated Approach* is subject to the terms of the following License Agreement and Limited Warranty.

Technical Support

Prentice Hall does not offer technical support for any of the programs on the CD-ROM. However, if the CD-ROM is damaged, you may obtain a replacement copy by sending an email that describes the problem to:

disc_exchange@prenhall.com.

IBM License Agreement

Instructions

The CD-ROM accompanying this book contains IBM material. You will be shown the following license agreement when you click on links to access this material on the CD. A "Download now" button is available at the bottom of the license agreement window; pressing the button signifies that you agree with the license agreement and allows you to access the material. If you disagree with the license agreement, close the window to return to the main page.

The license agreement window also includes information about how to acknowledge IBM for the use of these materials.

License Agreement

THIS IS A LEGAL AGREEMENT BETWEEN YOU (EITHER AN INDIVIDUAL OR AN ENTITY) AND THE IBM CORPORATION. BEFORE DOWNLOADING OR USING THE CODE AND OR DOCUMENTATION (HEREINAFTER "MATERIAL"), YOU SHOULD CAREFULLY READ THE FOLLOWING TERMS AND CONDITIONS. DOWNLOADING OR USING THE MATERIAL INDICATES YOUR ACCEPTANCE OF THESE TERMS AND CONDITIONS. IF YOU DO NOT AGREE TO THE TERMS AND CONDITIONS OF THIS AGREEMENT, DO NOT DOWNLOAD OR USE THE MATERIAL. THE MATERIAL IS OWNED BY IBM, ITS SUBSIDIARIES (IBM), OR IBM_S SUPPLIERS, AND IS COPYRIGHTED AND LICENSED (ACCORDING TO THE TERMS AND CONDITIONS ENUMERATED BELOW), NOT SOLD. IBM RETAINS TITLE TO THE MATERIAL.

I. GRANT OF LICENSES.

Subject to the terms and conditions of this Agreement, IBM grants to you the non-exclusive, non-assignable, royalty free and fully paid-up license, under the applicable IBM copyrights, to:

1. use, execute, display, perform, and reproduce, the Material;
2. prepare derivative works based on the Material;
3. distribute copies of the Material and derivative works thereof; and
4. authorize others to do all of the above, provided they agree to the terms and conditions of this Agreement.

You may not copy, modify or merge copies of the Material except as provided in this Agreement. You may not rent, lease, sell, sublicense, assign, distribute or otherwise transfer the Material except as provided in this Agreement. You may not reverse compile or reverse assemble any part of the Material which is provided in object code form.

You may not sell, transfer, assign, or subcontract any of your rights or obligations under this license. Any attempt to do so is void.

You must reproduce the copyright notice and any other legend of ownership on each copy or partial copy of the Material and derivative works thereof.

IBM would appreciate receiving a copy of derivative works of the Material that You create. You may provide to IBM such derivative works pursuant to the terms of this Agreement. You represent and warrant to IBM that You are the sole author of, and/or have full exclusive right, title and interest to any and all derivative works You provide to IBM. You further represent that You are under no obligation to assign your rights in such derivative works to any third party, including without limitation, any current or former employer.

With respect to any derivative works of the Material You provide to IBM, You grant to IBM an irrevocable, worldwide, non-exclusive, perpetual, royalty-free and fully paid-up license to:

1. use, execute, display, perform, and reproduce, the Material;
2. prepare derivative works based on the Material;
3. distribute copies of the Material and derivative works thereof; and
4. authorize others to do all of the above.

You agree that any information or feedback you may provide to IBM in reference to the Material or this Agreement is non-confidential and you grant IBM a worldwide, fully paid up and irrevocable license to use this information/feedback without restriction.

II. DISCLAIMER OF WARRANTY.

THE MATERIAL IS PROVIDED "AS-IS". IBM MAKES NO WARRANTIES OF ANY KIND, EITHER EXPRESS OR IMPLIED, WITH RESPECT TO THE MATERIAL. IBM EXPRESSLY DISCLAIMS THE IMPLIED WARRANTIES OF MERCHANTABILITY AND FITNESS FOR A PARTICULAR PURPOSE AND ANY WARRANTY OF NON-INFRINGEMENT. THE ENTIRE RISK ARISING OUT OF USE OR PERFORMANCE OF THE MATERIAL REMAINS WITH YOU.

Some jurisdictions do not allow the exclusion of implied warranties or the exclusion or limitations of consequential or incidental damages, so the above provisions relating thereto may not apply to you.

IBM has no obligation to provide service, defect correction, or any maintenance for the Material. IBM has no obligation to supply any Material updates or enhancements to you even if such are or later become available.

Under no circumstances is IBM liable for any of the following:

1. third-party claims against you for losses or damages;
2. loss of, or damage to, your records or data; or
3. direct damages, lost profits, lost savings, incidental, special, or indirect damages or other consequential damages, even if IBM or its authorized supplier, has been advised of the possibility of such damages.

Neither of us may bring any legal action more than two years after the cause of action arose.

Note to U.S. Government Users - Documentation related to Restricted Rights — use, duplication, or disclosure is subject to restrictions set forth in GSA ADP Schedule Contract with IBM Corporation.

This Agreement is entered into in the State of New York, U.S.A. and governed by the laws of the State of New York without regard to conflict of law principles. Regardless of where you access this Program from, you agree to comply with all applicable United States laws including those regarding export of data.

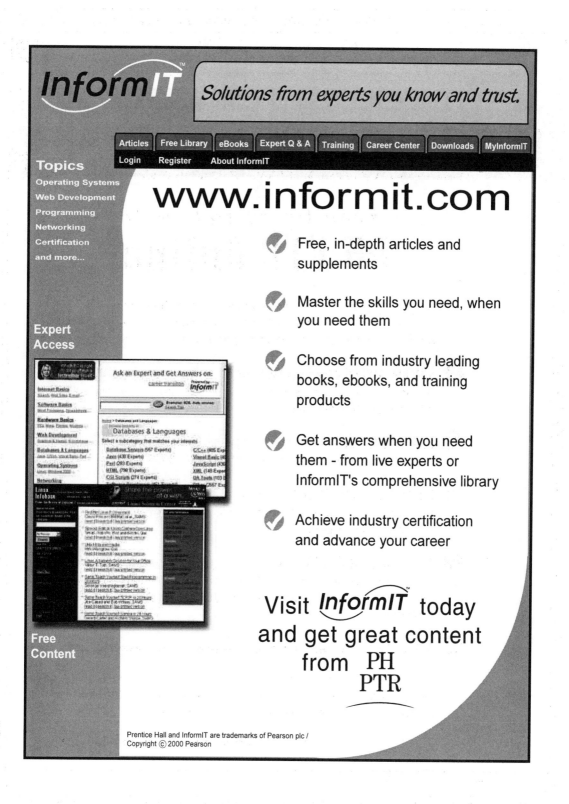

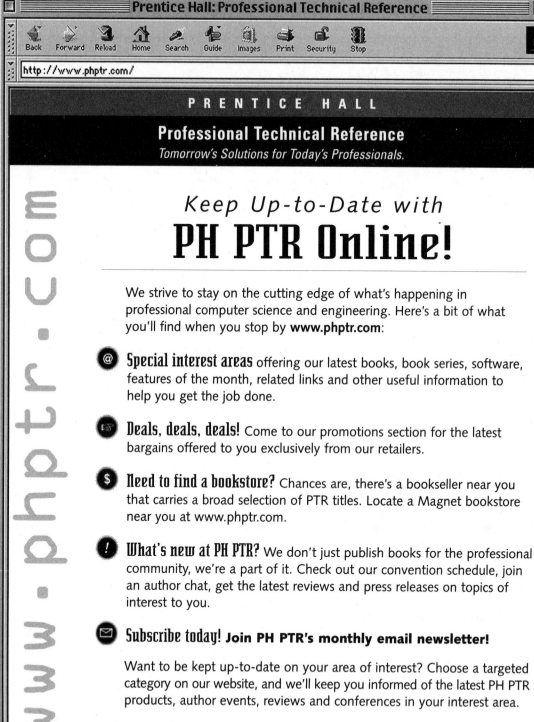

SOFTW

PRACTICAL SOFTWARE ENGINEERING SERIES